River of Memories

Roger Aggett

A personal recollection of Noss Mayo

Regatta day in August about 1910.
The spirit of the festive occasion so many years ago is captured in this photograph showing the *Princess Royal* paddle-wheel steamer behind the funnel of which can just be seen the smaller *Kitley Girl* steamer. The two boats in the foreground are a Plymouth hooker and a house boat called *Lamorna*. Races appear to be taking place in the background.

This version of the book is virtually as originally published, presenting the work of Roger Aggett. There are now additional pages at the back providing information about the publisher, Arthur L Clamp.

The republishing project is being managed by Arthur's grandson, Steven Gibson. We aim to find all the research that he was involved in publishing, preserving it for the next generation as part of 'The Clamp Collection'.

Words of Thanks

My mother, Miriam Aggett, her parents and grand parents were born and lived out their lives in the village of Noss Mayo. My grandfather, George Hodge, senior, was the skipper on Lord Revelstoke's steam pinnace *Wasp* which ran a ferry service between Newton, Noss and Millbay Docks, Plymouth, weather permitting, bringing goods and guests to the estate at Membland. Soon after the trains started running in the late 1890s he started the ferry service between Steer Point and the three villages of Wembury, Newton Ferrers and Noss Mayo.

My grandmother's mother died when she was very young. Grandma Hodge was brought up by Uncle Joe Penwell and his wife Sarah at the *Globe Inn*. Uncle Joe organised the runs to deliver the smuggled goods out of the Yealm area; most of the fishermen at that time were also engaged in some degree of smuggling.

In the days before radio and television we young people would congregate at No. 50 Noss Mayo where Grandma Hodge was a good story teller talking about smugglers when she was a young girl or read to us by the light of a paraffin lamp on the kitchen table. Before my mother died in 1960 many Sunday afternoons were spent going around the farms and the old Membland estate. From them both I learnt much about the old days at Noss.

Many thanks are extended to John Rowsell, Jack Nicholson, John Hockaday, Michael Leonard and others. Jean and Harry Hockaday have been very kind in accommodating myself and my wife Irene for many summer vacations taken in writing and research for this publication and for providing many old photographs.

The *River of Memories* is thought to describe accurately short stories of village life in the parish of Revelstoke prior to 1980. Special thanks to my American wife Irene and her friend Joan Westfall in helping me to typescript these pages ready for the printer.

Roger Aggett,
Carradale, Passage Road,
Noss Mayo, Near Plymouth
PL8 1EW March 2001.

Roger Aggett proudly displays his cups in 1950. He went to work at Salcombe in 1946 and remained there for eighteen years maintaining a keen interest in boats both for business and pleasure. He was also secretary of the Salcombe Sailing Club for part of his stay.

A Short History of Noss

A map of the area encased in a glass frame by the recreation hall (Chapel of Ease later Noss school) states *Noss Mayo is first mentioned in the thirteenth century when the perimeter from the Pool around to Stoke belonged to Matthew Fritz Herbert. It was known as Nosse de Matthieu from which came Noss Mayo.*

Both sides of Noss creek being steep the villagers had to quarry into the soft red shale rock then using the rock to build the houses and roads. No mean task in those days before machinery. Since the church registers only go back as far as 1654 it is not known when the village was first settled. An early record found at Exeter dated 1625 stated *Sir John Hele purchased a house and garden for £25 with money left over for the use of the poor.* The location is not stated but is thought to be near Noss.

There is very little written history about the village of Noss Mayo. The main occupations were fishing and farming; the village was self-supporting regarding food. Most other goods were ferried from Plymouth by boat.

The parish of Revelstoke, containing 1,654 acres, was not founded until 1654. The parish registers were started thirty-nine years later. The earliest tradesmen's directory located is dated 1820, these directories only list the farmers and tradesmen in the parish, no history.

Tilley Institute once the National Board School

The Tilley Institute was the first Noss school. This building, once known as the National Board School, was built in 1839. It consisted of one large school room heated by a single fireplace. The school master's house adjoining is part of the same building. The school building costs were shared with a government grant and public subscription. The school cost £375 and the running expenses at that time were met by public subscription and fees from pupils.

Harold B. Plant, an ex-naval officer who had lost a hand, was the first master. The second was William Cann. In 1878 Edward Charles Baring of Membland Hall paid for an additional room to the school, installed a gas lighting plant and donated a library of 600 books. There is a forgotten statue of him in this room. This building, now known as the Tilley Institute, was given to the village by Sir William Gray as a memorial to Colonel Charles Tilley who was the land agent for many years for the Membland estate. He lost his life on 14th April, 1918, in the First World War. The Chapel of Ease, later becoming the second Noss school, is now the village recreation hall.

Chapel of Ease

The near derelict church at Stoke being over two miles from the village, the Chapel of Ease was built in 1839 costing £925. It was capable of seating 320 persons and had a gallery, chancel and vestry and an outside turret bell and clock. The dead had to be taken to Stoke for burial and marriages had to be performed at Stoke until 1862.

There are several forgotten graves in the orchard at the back of the chapel, some burials taking place before 1882 when the new church was consecrated. Old Stoke church was known as the chapel of St. Peter. Construction dates about it have been lost. The early priests were probably roman catholic monks from the priory near Holbeton. Most of these were closed in the reign of Henry VIII during the dissolution of the monasteries in the 1530s. after which St. Peters was served by curates from the church of England at Yealmpton.

Fourteen years after the Chapel of Ease was built in the village the Bishop of Exeter purchased four acres of land at the top of the old Stoke road from the Rev. Sir John Perring of Membalnd Hall upon which was built a rectory. The first vicar for the parish of Revelstoke was the Rev. Kestral Cornish from 1861 to 1866. The second was the Rev. John Otto West from 1866 to 1871. The third vicar at Noss was the Rev. Henry F. Rowe, 1871 to 1890. In his autobiography Maurice Baring relates that he had to attend church with his parents taking a book to read because the morning service started at 11 a.m. continuing until 1 p.m.

Cholera Epidemic

The tradesman's diary at Exeter dated 1850 stated that 613 people were living in the parish of Revelstoke. From the same source can be read *Crab, lobsters, herring and other fish are caught at Noss Mayo where the villagers suffered severely from cholera in 1849 when around fifty of them died and more than 200 were affected with the dreadful malady. Liberal subscriptions were made for the relief of the sufferers and a medical gentleman was sent down from London to their assistance.*

Because the fever was so contagious a barn close to the two stone-built houses by the pathway at Hannaford was used as a hospital. Most of the dead were buried at Stoke. I was told that skipper Hodge's father, Richard, a healthy fisherman aged thirty, helped carry a friend to Stoke for burial. That same evening he was taken ill and within a week he was also buried at Stoke. His headstone bears the date 7th June, 1849.

Methodist Chapel

There used to be two old ruined cottages on the site where the chapel was built in 1870. The Foster family, all fishermen at that time, have been involved with the chapel since it was built with several generations of Fosters playing the organ. It could be heard throughout the village on calm Sunday mornings.

For many years a prominent farmer of Irish descent from Newton Ferrers attended morning services always immaculately dressed in tweeds, white shirt and necktie wearing well polished brown boots.

The Methodist ministers were rotated weekly. On many occasions the congregation and the preacher were captivated by this well dressed farmer standing up to loudly argue a religious point with the minister.

St. Peter's Church, Revelstoke

The 1st Lord Revelstoke foreseeing the need for a new village church and burial ground commissioned the eminent church architect, Mr. J. P. St. Aubyn, to design a church to complement Holy Cross across the creek at Newton Ferrers. Mr. George W. Crosbie was in charge of the masonry work. Henry Hems of Exeter was responsible for the ornate carvings and the beautiful interior oak woodwork.

The church took a little over two years to build. Although not quite completed, the Bishop of Exeter consecrated the building and land in 1882 this being the gift to the parish by Edward Charles Baring, 1st Lord Revelstoke. In the same year the chapel of ease became the Church of England school. One of the new school masters was the parish vicar, the Rev. W. E. Roome, M.A., 1890 to 1922, who had earned his degree at Corpus Christi College, Cambridge. He taught at Noss for almost twenty-two years.

Some Interesting Cottages

When Edward Baring purchased the Membland estate on the 25th August, 1871, the estate included all the parish of Revelstoke and the village of Noss Mayo with many acres in the parish of Holbeton as well. His son, Maurice, writes that the village consisted of white-washed thatched cottages and that his father rebuilt many of them with Devonshire stone and slate roofs.

Houses Nos. 3 and 4, Point side, are very old interesting cottages. They each had a down stairs living room with an iron stove for heating and cooking. In order to reach the single upper bedroom one had to exit the front door and enter the bedroom by a back door at the higher level.

No. 50 is also an interesting old house. The ceiling beams in the kitchen came from planks of an old ship. There used to be a door at the back of the parents' bedroom leading to another bedroom. This was the only entrance to the daughter's bedroom, good planning for those days.

The *Olde Ship*, formerly *The Globe*, is an old structure. Unfortunately it has been extensively altered with additions to the south side. There are two very interesting ceiling beams in the children's bar. They are full of borings indicating part of a ship's planking attacked by a sea worm known as a "gribble".

No. 39 Noss, a very old house, has a beautiful lower room on the south side, the wood flooring slopes towards the road, the beamed ceiling and doorway are very low.

Nos. 52 and 53 Noss are relatively new houses which were built by Lord Revelstoke.

Smuggling

Almost everyone fishing out of the Yealm at one time was a smuggler. It was the usual practice for a fisherman to barter his catch of fresh fish for a few luxury goods being brought to England by small sailing ships whose crew had lived on salt pork for weeks. Between 1600 and 1900 the majority of the working classes were very poor earning low wages with large families to support.

The government could not tax these people and in order to tax the wealthy an excise duty (custom duty) tax was imposed on numerous so called luxury goods such as sugar, pepper, spices, tea, coffee, brandy, wines and spirits and all tobacco products. Also taxed were silk, cotton, tapestries, lace and all imported cloth.

The old sailing ships, usually owned by the captain and a few wealthy gentry ashore, used to have to buy their cargo overseas to ship home and sell. When a vessel was expected it was usual for the gentry to alert a few fishermen to bring some of the cargo ashore so enabling owners to escape paying the duty at the dockside.

The Yealm river was ideal having eighty fishing vessels and over 200 fishermen. The villagers at Noss owned at least twenty donkeys to transport the goods. The donkeys were kept at the back of the old Church of England school.

When I was young many of us used to sit around Grandma's Hodge's chair in the kitchen at No. 50, lit by the dim light of an oil lamp on the table, listening in awe to her tales of the smugglers. She always said that Uncle Joe Penwill was a smuggler. They lived above the *Globe Inn* (*The Olde Ship*). Many years ago when modifications were being made to the inn a false wall with a cavity of 3 ft. behind was removed from a bedroom. Her stories related that most of the smuggled goods were hidden on the farms before delivery was made to the owners. Tomb stones at Stoke, Newton and Holbeton give some indication of the number of wealthy people and sea captains who lived in the area.

The last story about smuggling was in August, 1938. A wealthy Newton gent owning a 60 ft. motor yacht, *Harpado*, visited the Channel Islands. The captain, a well known Noss resident, an uncle of mine, brought a few bottles of the "good stuff" ashore taking great care to hide it in the old ivy-covered wooden shed in the back garden which had at one time housed the thunder bucket. A few weeks later he went to sample a bottle and found, according to his daughter, that her mother had emptied them all into the garden.

2nd Lord Revelstoke (1863-1929)

John Baring, eldest son of Edward Baring, who inherited Membland estate after his father's death in 1897, did not have the same passion for building as his father nor did he enjoy the close contact with the villagers. Charles Tilley, his agent, handled most of the affairs of the estate. John visited Membland less frequently than his father and spent more time in London. He always returned for the fox hunting and pheasant shooting and often spent Christmas at Membland. He is buried with his parents in St. Peter's churchyard.

Local Emigrants

Without the building programme of his father life at Noss began to stagnate. About 1909 Will Payne, a local man who had served in the merchant navy, was so sea sick that he left his ship in Canada. After a year or so he wrote home to his friends and parents about the good life he was enjoying in that country. His father was the white-bearded "Boss" Payne who with his wife Lena were the caretakers of the reading room, known now as the Tilley Institute.

My uncle Jack Hodge, after working long mornings in his brother's bake house, delivered bread with *Trixie*, the pony, and cart to Newton. His close friend Charlie Axworthy, a stone mason, was finding it difficult to get steady work and he became restless.

Finally Jack Hodge, Charlie Axworthy, Fred Foster, Bill Mashford, Stanley Penwill, Will Popham and Dick Light decided to emigrate. It was either 1911 or 1912. Mrs. Rowe, the vicar's wife, gave a farewell party at the school. In her speech she emphasied the importance of writing home regularly. The young men sailed from Plymouth the next day for Nova Scotia.

Will Payne was employed wheat farming on the vast praries. He had met with success due to his natural ability to work and to repair farm machinery.

On arriving in Canada the young men scattered. Jack Hodge and Charlie stayed together finding employment on a halibut fishing schooner which was owned by a Norwegian emigrant.

When the Great War started in 1914 Jack and Charlie joined the Canadian Infantry. Although they landed in Plymouth they did not get a chance to see their families at Noss being shipped to France the following morning. However, they met with Lionel Rowe from Noss in the trenches near the Somme. A few weeks later Charlie wrote to Jack's parents telling them that he had seen Jack who was wounded on a stretcher being carried to the rear by two German prisoners of war. Jack died of his wounds and is buried in France. A short time later Charlie was posted "missing in action". He has no known grave. Stanley Penwill was in the Canadian Mounted Rifles. He was killed near Arras in April, 1917. Nothing is known about William Popham who was also killed in France.

Will Payne survived the war and had moved to British Columbia where he built up a large automobile garage and dealership. He returned to visit Noss in the early 1950s. His mother, Lena May, was over eighty years of age and had not seen her son since he was eighteen years of age. I think it was 1945 when Dick Light returned to Noss but he never went back to Canada. I do not know how the rest of the emigrants fared.

The First World War 1914-18

When this war started most of the villagers joined the forces. Membland and surrounding areas were turned into an officers' training camp accommodating over 400 army cadets and training staff.

Skipper Hodge, who ran the ferry service to Steer Point to meet the trains with the steamers *Kitley Belle* and *Kitley Girl*, lost his crews. These steamers were close to 58 ft. long each carrying about eighty persons including the crew. The skipper steered from an exposed position in the bows. The engineer had to answer to a bell telegraph and see what was needed by putting his head out of the engine room window.

Coal for the vessels were wheeled in a hand cart almost half a mile from Steer Point railway halt. It was bagged and put aboard the *Loyalty*, a heavy 16 ft. rowing boat which was built by Tom Aggett, before it could be off-loaded into one of the steamers at the end of the day. The fare from Noss to Steer Point was 2d., later raised to 3d., takings being mostly in copper pennies which were carried home in a bucket after the last trip of the day.

Days were long and work was hard especially at low tide at Steer Point. The loaded vessels had to be helped off the beach using a pry bar. Because of baggage the trains had to be met with a hand cart.

Skipper's sons, Elliot Hodge and brother Ern, joined the navy as engineers on fast patrol boats based at Dover. George skippered a navy tug boat. To keep this ferry operating during the war years Lionel Baker and Vince Hodge, nephews, had to leave school before they were fourteen. My mother, Miriam Hodge, and sister-in-law, Queenie Hodge, and other family members worked on the two boats which ran from 6.30 a.m. to 11 p.m. seven days a week.

Spy Story

In 1911 Max Schultz landed in Plymouth. He was a regular officer receiving money from Ostend. A friendly relationship blossomed with Miss Sturgeon, his Plymouth landlady. They became well known entertaining guests lavishly at the Royal Palm and Royal Hotel at Plymouth.

One June they hired the yacht *Egret*, moored in the Yealm from a retired naval officer named Broughton living at Brunswick Cottage, Stoke. Life was going well for Max until he accidentally shot his lady friend in the shoulder. After she was taken to Greenbank hospital the authorities became interested in him. A secret service agent, Major

Gen. Sir Vernon Kell, and the local police raided the *Egret* finding letters and secret codes which enabled them to decode the many telegrams received and sent by Max. Thirty-one year old Max was tried under the Official Secrets Act at Exeter and was sentenced to twenty-one months in jail.

After the 1914-18 War

Soon after the war ended Sam Mashford and family, who for many years ran the ferries and the two barges carrying hundreds of tons of bricks from Steer Point to the Plymouth Cattewater, moved to the Saltash area and started a boatyard.

In 1921 the population at Noss was 466 persons. Fishing boats had been neglected during the war. There were only about twenty that were fishing. There was full employment on the farms each needing ten to twelve men. It was a false economy, wages were low. Most people worked ten hours a day for six days a week for under 35s.

The gardens were tilled. Everyone had poultry, the cockerels awakening the villagers each morning. Water still had to be carried from various taps situated around the village. We bathed in a tin tub each Saturday night. Each household had a small outhouse with a thunder bucket where newspapers were read for a second time in this library. It was not a disgrace to wear patched clothes or darned socks.

Yet Noss was a happy place. I grew up with such characters as Jumbo, Shackey, Fido, Chow, Scalley, Bonzo, Scewchy and my name was Ginge. These nick names were not family orientated but a hand down from the smuggling days when people concealed their true identity. We played weak horses, relieval and foxhounds.

Ye Olde Original Store

Foster's shop one was of the very early village structures complete with a thatch roof. George Harry Foster, a local fisherman, purchased the shop in 1894 from William Roberts. It was run by Miss Hettie Foster and George's wife Bessie. Besides all kinds of groceries this shop sold pots and pans, rope, fishing tackle, etc. It was also the post office. The other store at Noss being Vince Hodge's grocery and bake house at Point side.

Johnny Walters, a Plymouth man, built the new store next to the *Swan* in the early 1920s. Note the round-topped alcove over the tap. After the cholera epidemic a brick reservoir was built at Hannaford. This fed water, I believe, to seven public taps in the village. This drinking water had to be carried in buckets to the houses and was then boiled in black iron gallon kettles on the old black Lidstone grates used summer and winter in most households.

Pillory Hill

This is so named because of the pillory or whipping post which stood at the top of the hill used for many year as a form of public punishment prior to 1829 when Sir Robert Peel brought some kind of order to law enforcement. Before this date the villain was tried by the local Justice of the Peace who was often the Lord of the Manor.

If found guilty he was sentenced to a number of lashings with the "cat of nine tails", a leather whip with nine knotted throngs. Lesser offenders received lashings with the birch, a bunch of twigs tied together. The punishments were administered by the local constable who was often a local bruiser appointed to keep the peace.

In Grandma Hodge's youth the stocks were used to replace the pillory, the poor offender having to sit locked in a very uncomfortable position for some hours. For many years the stocks were kept in the porch of Noss church.

Children's Pastimes

We had snail races marking out a course on slate stones which bordered almost every house in Noss. We found the succulent crustaceans among the ivy. It was a most aggravating sport because the snails would hide in their shells and to get them motivated along a track we had to wet a path for them. This ancient sport usually ended by a disgusting competitor snorting down a snot and gobbing it on the race track.

In 1920 Johnny Walters built a shop at the bottom of Pillory Hill, post office stores. Later we kids often took turns in cranking the ice cream machines in the early mornings. We were never given a half penny cone, only the joy of licking the blades after most of the ice cream was scraped off.

In the 1920s no love was lost between the Newton and Noss boys. If one or two Noss boys tried to cross the Voss to Newton there was often a mud fight which ended in blows, the Newton crowed being led by a boy called Lapthorn. He lived in a shop where the yacht club is now. This brought village boys at Noss together.

When Victor Butterworth gave Jim Hodge an old bicycle we shared it and most of the village boys learnt to ride it. After the chain broke and the tyres worn out it was known as the "bone shaker" and had many proud owners until it was completely worn out.

We lived through periods when we chased hoops through the village, cutting down young ash branches in Paige's woods to make bows and hunted for straight twigs to make arrows. We would scudder stones on the water, many throwing a flat one the fifty-eight yards across Noss creek.

Owning Rowing Boats

Most families owned a rowing boat. We could row almost as soon as we could walk. Minnie Lancaster, the school mistress, gave us swimming lessons at an early age. No one got into trouble. Pollock could be caught almost anywhere in the Pool. We young fishing experts used to watch Lawrence Williams, a happy chubby man, always wearing a cloth cap which when raised showed a white line between his hair and rugged complexion. Lawrence had a 14 ft. tarred rowing boat with the ever popular Revelstoke blue top plank. He used to scull the boat towing two lines attached to short twiggs. These were constantly twitching and he would be hauling in fish, often to our dismay when he was close to us as we were patiently waiting for a bite.

Memories of being Young

We had plenty to do with spending afternoons in the harvest fields walking behind the binder, chasing rabbits when they bolted and piling up the sheaves of corn to dry. Many happy relaxing days were spent up and down Kitley river on the old *Pioneer* to Steer Point.

In the autumn weeks were spent collecting brush and rubbish for the bonfire on the playground for the 5th November. Another great event was the small fair coming to Noss every year until a gale brought high tides and almost washed it away.

There were a few poachers among us, some having wire snares and nets to trap rabbits when they bolted after being smoked out from the hedge rows.

Many enjoyable evenings were spent at the bottom of Pillory Hill wagering among ourselves as to which car would fail to make it to the top. We used to enjoy the sports car hill climbs which often took place in the steep muddy lane which ran up the back of Paige's farm. Passengers would leave their seats to bounce up and down on the rear bumper.

Arrival of the Steamers

In the latter half of the 1920s Noss was becoming known to the outside world. The large paddle-wheel steamers, *Princess Royal* and *Princess Alexandra* along with the *Kitley Belle* and *Pioneer*, were bringing hundreds of visitors to Noss and Newton. People were walking around the scenic drive and to Membland to view the ruins.

At least six tea gardens opened at Noss and were doing a roaring trade on fine summer weekends. Eight ferrymen were carrying passengers ashore in rowing boats at the Pool. Hodge's bakery started making fruit and ginger cakes and Mrs. Paige, at the dairy, was making many extra pounds of clotted cream.

Stoke Beach

Sometime in the 1920s the Plymouth Co-op started selling ice cream and minerals at Stoke House. The flat land below was becoming a tent city. Many campers, well tanked up at the *Globe Inn*, celebrated their return to Plymouth on the last bus which left at 9.50 p.m. carrying an inspector as well as a conductor. By 1930 the world recession had started and the paddle wheel steamers from Plymouth stopped running and the railway to Steer Point and Yealmpton was closed.

More Youthful Memories

Dick Rowsell came to Noss as its chief coastguard in 1927. There were four girls and three boys in the family. It was about 1930 when John, the youngest, and I became friends. Owen, an older brother of John, showed us lads how to make catapults from a forked branch and using rubber cut from an old shoe. This ingenious contraption was tied together with string.

Our ammunition was a pocketful of pebbles taken from the road close to Battery Cottage. Many happy days were spent among the bracken under the drive firing at anything that moved. We were true frontiersmen, our only trophies being a few seagull eggs which were often cracked open on a rock and slurped down.

We used to fish the rocks around Gara Point often catching as much fish as we could carry home. John's father would lend us his boat when we were all about eleven years of age provided we stayed inshore of Mouthstone Ledge.

Many happy days were also spent at Silver Sands at low tide John digging furiously and me catching the sand eels, etc. or vice versa. We had a fifty-hook bolter which we used to bait with the eels and set just outside the Bar. With the remaining bait we fished for pollock. It was not unusual for us to catch over two buckets full of fish in a morning.

This boat had a centre-board case. We had aspirations of being yachtsmen. My worldly wealth consisted of pennies and half pennies kept in a red tin box. Taking this wealth I went to the Mayflower Sailing Club in Plymouth hoping to buy a sail. Jimmy Hocking, a retired trawler skipper, took pity on me and sold me an old gray mildewed mainsail of about 80 sq. ft. It was soaped and scrubbed but it stayed a light shade of gray. A piece of blue ribbon was found and our No. 1 racing number was sewn on the sail.

We hit a problem. Father Dick would not let us have the iron centre-board, rightly thinking that we would capsize and sink. We had a sail and a boat but nothing else.

First we needed a mast. John went wooding and cut off the top of a fir tree. We found that the bottom of our mast had too big a diameter to enter the hole in the mast thwart. George Harvey, a dockyard worker who used to weekend on a small cabin cruiser in the Pool, came to our aid with a big knife and peeled off the low areas of bark and wood until the mast fitted the hole. He also sawed the bottom of the mast to fit the step.

About that time someone stole my mother's clothes line, blocks and ropes. We could splice rope but knew nothing about splicing wire. One of us held the wire with a tool while the other twisted the eye by means of a screw driver in the loop. We were beginning to win. Captain Rob Hodge loaned us an old spar for the gaff or yard. We were now bankrupt, clean out of money, so I went digging and selling worms and went from door to door trying to sell pollock.

A trip to Woolworths purchased three galvanized blocks at 3d. each and a 6d. clothes line for our main sheet. We scrounged an old rudder off Elliot Hodge and a 3 ft. length of used 1 inch pine floor board off Jack Payne, the local builder, for a dagger board. With a little more scrounging we had our yacht together. We were natural sailors, fortunately never capsizing.

We sailed the Yealm for about three years before the old sail started rotting through use. The fish we caught was never wasted. We kept them fresh by frequently wetting an old sack on top of the fish box which we carried under the after seat. During the summer months fish were eaten almost daily.

Yealm United Football Team

The team always had a good following. The annual match between Noss and Newton was an important event. One year before the Second World War the teams met on a field belonging to Captain Glyn Percy, the owner of Beacon Hill Estate at Newton. After the match the two tired teams lined up facing each other standing to attention.

A very attractive, well-dressed young lady passed between the ranks pinning on medals. Newton received gold medals, Noss silver. These were the envy of every aspiring young footballer until the medals were found to be copper pennies of that time. Some were painted gold and were glued to a piece of coloured ribbon looped over a safety pin.

The 1930s

This decade was not too good at Noss. Tractors were beginning to cause unemployment on the farms and by now the crabbers were gone. Lawrence Williams was still fishing from a rowing boat. Harold Sims had a 14 ft. boat with an outboard engine still crabbing. Bill Leonard and son Everette were fishing from their new boat *Atlantic*.

Bill had fallen as a boy damaging a knee. His leg was permanently bent. He was never without his single crutch ashore. At sea he balanced himself leaving both hands free to haul crab pots by putting his injured knee on a thwart.

Landel Leonard was one of Bill's two sons. He learnt boat building with Tom Agate who had acquired the Malt House and was busy building top quality boats when he died aged twenty-nine. Tom Algate, now getting on in years, was making a living by renting out his lovely light blue and chocolate-painted rowing boats with varnished spruce spoon-bladed oars. He also rented two nice safe sailing boats.

Elliot Hodge, assisted by his son Clarence (Jumbo), made a living painting and repairing yachts, building small boats and laying moorings in the river. By 1936 increasing numbers of villagers were travelling on the buses to work in Plymouth.

Tradesmen of Noss

Jim and Ivor Parsons, blacksmith
Mrs. Edmonds, confectionary
V. Hodge and Son, baker and grocer
Foster's shop, grocer and post office
Albert Pearson, shoe repair and taxi
Clarry Nicholson, market garden produce
Ralph Hockaday, green grocer and groceries
Victor Butterworth, marine engineer
Annie Cawse and sister, white laundry
Paige's dairy, milk, cream and eggs
George Mehan, Sunday newspapers, taxi, etc.
Fred Clark, family butcher
Lawrence Williams, fish and crabs
Harold Sims, crabs and lobsters
Vince Hodge, Swan Inn
Bob Scaddon, Globe Inn
Reg Doddridge, Plymouth carrier

George Adams, milk carrier
Iris Williams, daily newspapers
Tom Algate, boat builder and boat hirer
Elliot Hodge, moorings and boat building
Jack Payne, master house builder and repairs
Bob Baker, furniture maker
Mrs. L. Leonard, boat storage at Bridgend
Stan Crocker, boat storage, hair cutting, etc.
Bill Crook, baker, hair cutting
Henry Chaffe, Worsewell farm
Johnny Wakeham, Rowden farm
Mr. Rogers, Netton farm
Jack Northcott, ferryman
George Bevey, chimney sweep
Nona Croft, ladies dress making
Clump and Bert Revel, local carriers
Bill Tope, carpenter, boat builder

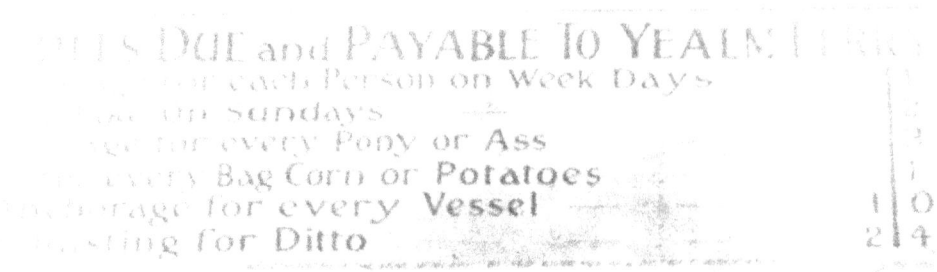

Ferry Boat Story

Skipper George Hodge, Sr., went to sea with his father crabbing and fishing when he was young. His father died in the cholera epidemic of 1849. The skipper inherited the boat and continued fishing living with his family above the *Globe (Ship Inn)* In 1887 when my mother was four years old the family moved to No. 50 Noss Mayo. After Edward Charles Baring, 1st Lord Revelstoke, purchased Membland Hall the skipper was hired to captain the *Wasp*, a forty foot steam pinnace.

There being very poor roads between Membland and Plymouth the *Wasp* was used as a year-round ferry bringing guests from the railway station, then at Millbay, and provisions for the household. Not much is known about this vessel except that she had a small wheelhouse, one steam engine and boiler. The aft cabin with upholstered seats was varnished.

Lord Revelstoke thinking he was doing the skipper a favour built Kiln Quay in 1884 with a boat house below to accommodate the *Wasp* and a small yacht belonging to his son John. Quite nice accommodation was built over the slipways. The skipper refused the accommodation preferring to stay at No. 50 Noss which had a large garden. He always kept two pigs and poultry, having a family of ten to feed. He and his boys always tilled the garden.

The skipper ran the *Wasp* for many years until the trains started running to Yealmpton and the new road was built. Revelstoke coaches, drawn by two horses, used to meet the trains at Yealmpton proceed up the new road to the Plymouth-Kingsbridge road to enter the Membland estate at the Bull and Bear gate. Newton Hill, the alternate route, was considered too steep for safety.

Before the railway was built the easiest was to reach Plymouth from the Yealm was by crabbing boat, taking about two hours rowing and sailing in favourable conditions. The alternative route was to take a ferry to Wembury, walking more than six miles over hilly country and narrow footpaths to Turnchapel then taking a ferry to the Barbican, a journey often taking three hours. Because of the poor roads the first carriers to make a return trip to Plymouth in one day were Harry Kimgcombe and William Hockaday.

The old iron railway bridge crossing the river Plym was built by the South Western Railway Co., to link Oreston to the main line services, the small village of Oreston in those days was busy with handling timber and quarried stone exports.

The Great Western Railway Co., built a six mile stretch of line connecting the L.S.W.R. line at Plymstock terminating at Yeampton with halts at Billacombe, Elburton, Brixton Road and Steer Point. The first train started at the Millbay railway terminus on 15th January, 1898. When the line first opened there were four round trips a day which soon increased to six through demand. The trains were carrying milk and farm produce to Plymouth as well as passengers. Huge stocks of coal were delivered to Yealmpton and other stops for the local coal merchants. The railway soon became an important undertaking for the area.

With the coming of the railway the *Wasp* had little use. His Lordship put the skipper to work on his estate but this was not to his liking. He had Tom Algate build him a 16 ft. rowing boat *The Royalty* and started, assisted by George, a son, to row a ferry service from Noss Mayo to Steer Point. Before too long the *Puffing Billy* arrived. She was similar to a 20 ft crabber having a steam engine with a vertical boiler. I think she was owned by Joe Hartnel and his son Sam, two Newton men. Before long a partnership was formed with the skipper he having half share. For several years the *Puffing Billy* was run towing *The Royalty* behind along with other boats if needed.

The skipper eventually bought out Joe Hartnel, procured a loan through Barings Bank, and had the *Kitley Belle* built by Hocking Bros., Cremyll Street, Plymouth, around 1905. She was powered by a 25 hp engine, was licensed by the Board of Trade to carry seventy-eight passengers and a crew of two. The skipper had it made until about 1914 when Sam Lugger arrived at the Yealm with an old Turnchapel ferry saying he was going to run the skipper off the river.

He named her *Kitley Girl*. Noss people, being faithful to the skipper, refused to board her so before too long the skipper took over the *Kitley Girl*. She was a problem vessel having only one boiler to feed two steam engines. She was only used as a standby and on busy summer weekends.

Shortly after the end of the 1914-18 war she was at Pope's Quay with the fire well stoked to get up a good steam pressure when she blew a boiler tube. She was never repaired and was moored off Brook for a time and later on the beach, Noss side, below Junket Corner, where Tom Algate had his boat shop. During one winter gale she broke adrift and on a sitch got holed at Bridgend. The skipper gave her to Bert and Clump Revell who broke her up.

Shortly after this the Yealm Hotel Co., purchased a steam pinnace named the *Yam Yam*. She was crewed by Joe and Dick West and Harry Moon. She had a large unprotected deck and small cabin accommodation.

The skipper sent his youngest son, Elliot, to find him another vessel. Elliot found the *Pioneer* at St. Mawes, near Falmouth. She was a 48 ft. well-built ferry boat having a three cylinder hot bulb type Gardener paraffin engine making her the fastest vessel on the Yealm. Before long the *Yam Yam* disappeared.

The skipper anticipating an end to the Steer Point ferry service in the winter months purchased two Ford lorry chassis round 1924 and had Mumfords of Plymouth convert them to buses to carry 15 passengers and a driver. They were basically lorries with four lines of seats across with a canvas top and side screens which were seldom fitted. The first was a failure, being too heavily built for the steep hills, the second was lighter and a little better. After a couple of years they were sold to the Devon Motor Transport Co., the forerunner of the Western National line.

In 1929 the Great Western Railway started a bus service meeting the trains at Yealmpton for Noss. In 1930 the trains stopped running and buses to Plymouth took over.

The *Kitley Belle* was moored off Wide Slip until 1933 when she was sold for £75 to the Milbrook Steanboat Co. who fitted her with a steering shelter and a new Gardener 6L2 diesel engine. For many years she ran the Millbrook to Mutton Cove, Devonport, ferry service and often took passengers to Cargreen and Calstock up the Tamar. She was commandeered by the Navy in 1940 and was used extensively in the Sound. At the end of the war she was sold to someone in Southhampton. Nothing more is known of her.

The *Pioneer* hung around the Yealm for many years. She was never given the engine she needed. Elliot Hodge broke her up in 1946, a good vessel wasted.

The skipper, George John Elliot Hodge died at the age of 78 in January, 1926. Apart from visits to Plymouth the furthest he ventured was one train journey to Southampton.

Kitley Belle Steamer.
This photograph was taken around 1915-20 and shows George Hodge, Jr., hauling up the anchor in readiness to take the lady passengers possibly up to Steer Point to catch the train into Plymouth. Note the buildings in the background showing the thatched roof of the *Dolphin Inn* at Newton.

The Finest Paddle Steamer.
The *Alexandra* is here on the Yealm about 1925 with passengers out for the day from Plymouth. The vessel was then owned by the Plymouth Piers, Pavilion and Saltash Three Towns Steamship Company. It was the largest boat sailing on the waters around Plymouth.

Puffing Billy
The first steam ferry seen here at Steer Point about 1900 transferring a passenger on journey to Noss.

Tamar Belle Steamer
A regular visitor to the Yealm from Plymouth with visitors to the estuary sometime in the 1930s. She was owned by the Millbrook Steamboat and Trading Company and was sold in 1929 to the King's Bargemaster, London. Three summer house boats are moored in the estuary. They are the *Diana*, *Shonita* and *Cerenia*.

An Overview of Noss Creek. A derelict sand barge lies in the centre of the creek, the *Kitley Belle* can just be seen moored at Pope's Quay and the *Globe Inn* was then run by George Lewis. The higher cottages have hardly changed whereas the waterfront dwellings have changed a lot. The period is around 1910.

Motor Vessel *Pioneer*
She is at Steer Point with George Hodge, Jr., assisting a passenger on board who has just alighted from the train. It is the late 1920s. This engine-driven vessel replaced the paddle steamer whose running costs were too high when coal prices rose through the 1926 general strike.

Last Visit.
This photograph records the last visit of the paddle steamer *Alexandra* in September, 1927, because of increasing fuel costs and the coming of petrol engines. She was built in 1888 and was scrapped at Cattedown after forty years of passenger service between the Yealm and Plymouth.

Arriving for Passengers.
It is about 1905 in Noss creek. The *Kitley Belle* will be taking on or alighting passengers to and from Steer Point. The crew were George Hodge, skipper, Ernest Hodge, engineer, George Hodge, Jr., deck hand and Elliot Hodge, general helper.

The *Pioneer* at Pope's Quay. Note the 18 inch wide gang plank used for boarding the vessel at low tides. The two wide double-ended vessels are ex-German lifeboats which the skipper purchased after the First World War. They were used for carrying goods from the train to Newton and Noss. By 1925 they were rusty and unsafe and were later towed to Wembury Bay and sunk.

Kitley Belle.
This well remembered vessel is here moored off Wide Slip sometime in the 1920s. It has all her five cabin windows opened, not a normal practice unless it is very hot.

Kitley Girl Steamer
This view of her is at high water in the creek but the date is not known. Built around 1887 she was sold to George Hodge around 1900. She was formerly the *Iolanthe*. Note that she had more windows than the *Kitley Belle*. She was laid up in 1930, broke her moorings during a storm and went aground at Bridgend where she was broken up.

Returning Plymouth. This view of the estuary captures the return of two ferry boats after a day's visit to the Yealm from Plymouth. Once a very common sight.

At Wide Slip in the 1920s. This interesting old photograph shows the pier in front of the Yealm Hotel, the lifeboat house with wide opening doors, the *Princess Royal*, the paddle steamer which made three daily runs in the summer months from the promenade pier below the Hoe at Plymouth. The smaller steamer is Hodge's *Kitley Girl*. There are three Yealm crabbers on the foreshore.

The Tea Cottage. It is thought that a Miss Read ran this for day passengers out from Plymouth on one of the many summer pleasure trips to the estuary. There were also tea gardens offering refreshments from a private house or garden ran by the lady of the family. The date is about 1910.

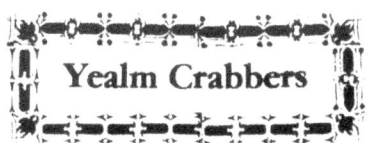

Yealm Crabbers

Times have changed, few people living at Noss go fishing. Pollock, once a favourite meal, is now despised shoppers preferring to bring fish home, filleted and nicely wrapped from supermarkets never giving a thought as to how and where the fish were caught.

The pollock, mackerel and whiting still abound but there are few bass which were always more difficult to catch. The chubb and bream which used to be caught at the Ebb Rocks have disappeared. Razor clams and hens can still be dug in the area where the beach joins the mud at the side of the stream running out of the fish-trap at Thorn. There are still clams to be dug on the sandy-mud shore at the top of the Kitley river. Scallops were found under the kelp by the baulking stores.

Conger eels up to 30 lbs. were often caught by the rafts situated opposite the Yealm Hotel after dark on an incoming tide with fresh mackerel used as bait. One has to look harder to find the small green crabs under stones on the beaches; excellent bait for bass and wrasse off the rocks.

The Kingcombe family fished the oyster beds in the Kitley river for many years. The oyster pond where the oysters were stored to cleanse themselves is now in ruins. Shrimp and prawns are still caught in the Pool.

There are now few part-time fishermen with a PH registration on the bows of their vessels. People seem to forget that at one time about 200 men in Newton and Noss made a living from fishing. Old fishing grounds and the feeding habits of fish are now almost forgotten memories.

Modern fishermen seem to think that fish have forsaken old haunts and now live in underwater mansions known as wrecks which cannot be found without the aid of Decca and a depth gauge.

Very few good pictures exist showing the original sprit-sail crabbers. There is a delightful old painting of the crabbers hung in the Tilley Institute showing them alongside old Pope's Quay.

The Pope brothers, both fishermen, were uncles of Mary Ann Pope (Grandma Hodge) the wife of skipper George Hodge, Sr., owner of the Kitley Belle Steamboat Co. which ran for twenty-seven years carrying passengers to the train at Steer Point.

For at least four generations the Hockaday family, who reside in the Round House, were the principal boat builders at Noss and were responsible for building most of the crabbers. The Round House is located on the road between Pillory Hill and Bridgend about 200 yards from the top of the hill. Before alterations were made this house had a large cellar. Boats up to 20 ft. long could be built in it and lowered over the bank into Noss creek.

The Hockadays also owned the triangular-walled piece of land where Point side joins the old school playground at the bottom of the village. The last clencher-built crabbers were built in this yard by William John Hockaday and his son Ralph before Ralph joined the army in the 1914-18 war.

Edgar Foster's *Thistle*.
It looks very much like this crabber has its sails specially raised for the photographer sometime in the 1930s. Mrs. Florence Foster is in the boat on the Yealm estuary. It was built at Salcombe in 1898 costing £14 and was the last crabber to sail out of the Yealm.

Snowdrop crewed by the Topes.
It is sometime in the 1930s in one of the many annual regattas and is in
the crabber Greyback race. Its crew are Jack Tope, cox., Bill Tope, stroke, Arch
Tope, Frank Tope and Gordon Tope. Numerous other boats are in the background.

Tom Algate and his son Tom were also boat builders whose shop still remains on the foreshore beneath Junket Corner. Tom Jr. built the only motor crabbber in 1929. She was built for Bill Leonard, carvel-planked, 22 ft. long and powered by a 2 cylinder Atlantic paraffin engine. This vessel, owned by the Leonard family, is still in use today.

The elm and oak used to build these boats were felled locally on the large Kitley estate. The trees were sawn by water power, one saw mill being at Pool Mill farm, the other near Snawdon's furniture factory located on the river Yealm near Yealmpton. The largest crabbers built at Noss were 20 ft. long. Designs were fairly standard being developed over the years. The Noss built boats were basically large open rowing boats with four thwarts, clenching built of wyche elm with an oak stem and keel, steam-bent oak ribs, all copper riveted and costing between £10 and £12.

All the crabbers had a sculling notch cut in the transom. The larger boats carried pig iron inside ballast with a short easily stowed mast, a foresail and a high-peaked sprit-rigged mainsail. They did not sail well to windward, a fisherman having to row on the lee side to help the vessel along. When the pots were being hauled the sails were lowered and the crabber rowed from pot marker to marker. It was a hard life. About once a week the catch was rowed or sailed to the Plymouth Barbican, about eight miles away, arriving before 7 a.m. to make the market.

Larger versions of the Yealm crabber, as it is now called, were built at Chant's boatyard, Salcombe, and at Dorman's next door. These boats averaged 22 ft. to 23 ft. long and were better designed for sailing having a deep wooden keel incorporating an outside iron keel. When they beached at low tide "scotches" were needed under the bilge to keep them upright. The open fishing boats were built at Salcombe because there was a good sawmill at hand and an iron foundry to cast the keels only four miles up the estuary at Kingsbridge. Their masts were short, not over 20 ft. long, easily stepped by one man at sea, being secured to the second thwart back from the bow by an iron hasp and supported by the two side stays.

There was a short iron bumkin permanently attached to the stem head, fitted with a bob stay. The rig was simple and efficient, the foresail being hooked onto the "ramshorn", a twisted piece of iron and hoisted. The mainsail was shaped from tanned canvas having an eye in each of the four corners and one set of reef points. This sail was hoisted on the mast and a spar, called a sprite, poked into the top after-corner of the sail. The bottom of the sprite was secured at gunwhale level to the mast by a rope-bound wire strop called a "snotter". The sail was loose-footed. After the first reef was taken in and a further reduction in sail area needed, the sprite was removed, the top corner tied to the mast making a triangular sail.

The author moved to Salcombe in 1946. Chant's boatyard was almost derelict with sheds falling down. Joey Chant, about 80 years old, was often pottering around. He loved to sit and relate how his father and grandfather built the trading ships which regularly crossed the Atlantic carrying a crabber as a lifeboat or towing gig because these trading ships did not have engines.

Dorman's boatyard also had seen better days. It was run by three brothers. Wilfred, over 80 years old, working alongside Aaron and Sydney, the youngest, who was always smartly dressed in a white shirt and yachting cap. The brothers were still building clencher boats of English wyche elm, very similar to the crabbers, they were now fitted with a 7 hp engine, the 13 cwt. iron keel no longer being fitted.

The brothers were very independent only working in warm weather rarely using the old paraffin engine circular saw. This was the only piece of machinery they possessed. The planking was sawn and planed by hand; they only built two or three boats a year.

When an order was placed the brothers would hold a conference. If they did not like the buyer's appearance they would turn down the order. George, a son, ran one of the motor crabbers for hook and line fishing. One evening I visited Dormans to buy some fish. The brothers were preparing to launch a new boat. I noticed a decided sweep in the varnished centre seat and on asking the reason why was told, "Well the Lawd grawed it that way and us thought it is a shame to alter it".

Jack Croker, an aged resident of Noss, was able to remember some of the crabbers. They were:

Fear Not owned by Joey Adams   *Emily* owned by Lawrence Williams
Minnie owned by Bob Lugger   *Shamrock* owned by Harry Hockaday
Freda owned by Sam Shepherd   *Coconut* owned by Jack Northcott
Emma Jane owned by Bill Leonard   *Eagle* owned by Harold Sims
Finch owned by Vince Hodge   *Thistle* owned by Edgar Foster
Snowdrop owned by Harry Foster   *May Queen* owned by George Light

The crabbing season started on Valentines's day, 14th February, ending just before Christmas. These crabbers fished using pots made of willows, most of the fishermen having willow plots in their gardens. There were also large willow plots by the old ferry landing and on the swampy piece of land opposite the two cottages at Coombe.

There was an unwritten territorial law amongst the local crabbers. East of the River Erme the grounds belonged to the crabbers from Bantham and Hope Cove. The *Yealmers*, as they were called, fished from the Erme as far west to the rocks between the Mewstone and Wembury. West of that line was Plymothians' territory. The Yealmers often shared the fishing on the East and West Rutts about three miles south-east of the Erme with the Hope Cove men who were "Methodist Chapelers" the same as most of the Noss men.

When Lord Revelstoke had the baulking stores built at Wembury he kept the top floor as a sail loft, the lower floor was rented to fishermen enabling them to store their gear and make up their crab pots and other fishing gear.

Besides the crabbers there were five herring drifters each about 35 ft. long. These vessels were very similar to the Looe drifters seen today. They carried a foresail, with main and mizzen masts each having a dipping lug sail. Each vessel carried a crew of four or five men spending several days at sea, fishing at night for herring and pilchards in Bigbury Bay or in the Channel offshore, excited gulls guiding them to schools of fish.

The catch was pickled in brine in casks and shipped to Plymouth. For some years a Portuguese trading vessel would arrive at the Yealm to load the casks. There were three small smoke houses now lost in the bracken at the top of Old Cellars beach. Besides being used for smoking fish the villagers often used these houses to smoke pork when a pig was killed. In addition to the crabbers and drifters there were also a few hookers. These vessels fished for mackerel in June, July and August, there being large schools in Bigbury Bay and in the Gulf Stream running about eighteen miles offshore.

When the mackerel season was over they fished with long lines stored in tubs, each holding 600 ft. of back line with about 180 stray lines with baited hooks. The fishing was continuous as fresh cut bait was necessary. If there was a shortage of bait when setting out one or two sets had to be made to catch enough small fish to bait up all the hooks. The *R.S.E.* was owned by Harry Hockaday. The *Little Aggie's* owner is forgotten. The *Ida* was owned by George Foster.

Young Boys of Noss.
It is fairly certain that boats fascinated most of the local boys seen in this group in Noss creek. It is probably the early 1930s, the *Globe* is in the right background and the boat PH272 is the *Thistle*, a crabber, owned by Edgar Foster.

Fishing on the *Ida*

George Foster, the owner of this boat, was a school friend of my mother. In the early thirties my brother and I started a long friendship with George and his brother Albert, spending many happy days with them fishing. The *Ida* was built at Looe in 1920 as a hooker and was now converted for crabbing. She still had the same mast but the mainsail was now cut off at the bottom and loose-footed. The foresail was also cut down, rarely used, being stored in the forward cuddy.

A 7 and a half hp poppit-valve Kelvin paraffin engine was installed with the propeller on the starboard side of the stern post. Mornings started at 6 a.m. usually taking half an hour to get the Kelvin started and warmed up. If the wind was helpful the mainsail would be raised and we headed for the East and West Rutts located by land marks.

We usually towed four mackerel lines and on arrival at the Rutts the gut and lures were exchanged for 10 ft. long wire leaders with either a black or red slow turning rubber worm. It was often my job to untwist a length of leader wire from a bicycle brake cable. After hauling mackerel for an hour it was great fun hauling three to eight pound pollock. If the tides were slack we drifted using mackerel for bait catching whiting.

As soon as we had hauled about 50 lbs. of bait we set course for the Erme taking care to miss the rock about half a mile offshore. Alan and I would help Albert haul the pots, remove the old bait and seaweed after he had removed the crabs and lobsters. The pots were heavy usually two on each string. George had a full-time job taking care of the *Ida*. We often fished within twenty feet of the rocks. If we started catching "five fingers" we would move the pots to a new area at least 200 yards away. We gradually worked our way back to Warren Point and then made for the Yealm after hauling around fifty pots.

Our average catch would consist of two or three conger eels, a dozen or so pouting and wrasse, thirty to forty lobsters and about fifty eating crabs with dozens of spider crabs which were given away. It was usually close to 5 p.m. before we put the crabs and lobsters in the store pots and cleaned up the boat. The *Ida* was the last boat fished by the Foster family who had worked out of the Yealm for many generations.

The Foster family, living in the house near Noss Voss with the cellar underneath, were all fishermen. They spent many cold nights at sea in open crabbers catching herring and pilchards. In the autumn the fishermen were often lucky in catching mullet. On quiet nights, often after good rain, mullet could be heard splashing in a creek near a swollen stream. Very quietly, fearful of spooking the fish, two men in a rowing boat would shoot a net around the school. Hauling the nets ashore from both ends it was not unusual to catch half a ton of fish. Judging by the size of the mullet in the Yealm no one has fished this way for many years

Two Tragedies

The approaches to the Yealm estuary are dangerous due to the many submerged rocks only showing at low water with strong tidal currents to carry slow moving fishing vessels off course. Fogs can be so thick that the bow of a vessel cannot be seen from aft. The fishermen of the Yealm must have been guided by divine providence because there are only three known losses to the large fishing fleet which once operated from here.

Just before Easter on 11th April, 1878, there were five crabbers at sea. The wind rapidly freshened to gale force from the south-west making it a fight to return to the Yealm from anywhere in Bigbury Bay. Three crabbers made it safely to harbour and as two were overdue the *Daring*, 35 ft. R.N.L.I. lifeboat, was launched with ten oarsmen straining she took a long time to clear the river entrance due to strong wind and breaking seas. After an extensive search in good visibility no trace of the missing crabbers were found.

At Point and at Low Water, pre-1914.
A very typical scene on the foreshore of Noss creek with a willow crab pot in the foreground, repair work likely taking place on the nearest boat and another rigged with a sprit and mainsail.

The lost crabbers were the *Seabird* and the *Mertle*. Dick West, 45 years old, with Alf Banks in one boat, Richard Jackson, 25 years old, and a Mr. Tucker were in the other boat. A few days after the gale one of the men's jerseys was washed up on the beach near Mothercombe. Part of one of the boats was washed up near Salcombe. Some days after this tragedy a Spanish vessel landed the body of one of the fishermen. He is interred in Newton churchyard.

The next tragedy is thought to have occurred in 1911. Aaron Axworthy had been fishing alone when his boat capsized returning over the Bar. Aaron could not swim because of his heavy sea boots. A search was made by many fishermen but to no avail. Next day one of the Mashford boys living in Ferry Cottage towing a line with a number of fish hooks caught him by the nose.

Besides the fishing fleet there were two large sailing barges operating out of the Yealm. They were crewed by men from the Mashford family some living in the village others at Ferry Cottage. The two barges, each about sixty ft. long were named *The Brothers* and *Provident*. They were trading barges delivering any cargo they were hired to carry. For many years they were the only reliable carriers to the Yealm unloading their cargoes on the small public quay by Ferry Cottage, The Mashfords never used Bridgend Quay because too much time was wasted towing the barges up the river and also his Lordship charged them a tariff.

The same family operated the public ferry from the same landing for several generations. Yealm is an old word to describe "soft, gentler water".

Providence Sailing Barge.
In the early years of the 1900s Captain Robert Mashford ran two barges, the other being *Two Brothers*, bringing in coal and other materials from Plymouth. This rare photograph shows *Providence* with probably Captain Mashford on board. He was assisted by one of his sons and the Yealm area was quite dependent on the reliability of these barges bringing in resources to the villages.

The First Crabber
She was built by Tom Algate at Bridgend for Bill Leonard who is at the rear of the boat. The three men to the left have not been be recognised in this 1930s photograph. The crabber was called *Atlantic* after her Atlantic paraffin engine. Two house boats are in the rear of the picture. Note the maun basket aboard.

Town or Noss side of the Creek in the 1920s.

This view from Point clearly shows the former fields and back gardens occupying most of the hillside with the tower of St. Peter's standing above them erected in 1880-81 and paid for by the 1st Lord Revelstoke. The author recalls many of the occupants of the cottages facing the creek. *Left to right*: In No. 53 Noss Mayo lived Elliot Hodge, No. 52 lived Ernest Hodge, Stan Crocker lived below the old boathouse, Bertie Harrison lived in No. 51, Grandma Hodge in No. 50, then came Nos. 49 and 48 owned by Mr. Bidgood, Silas Andrew was in No. 46 and ran a tea garden from here, Miss Shaw was in No.45. Mrs. Prynne lived in the small pitt box house and J. V. Dyer lived on the far right at water's level.

Starting a Fishing Trip.
The bait box gives the clue as to what is about to happen. Henry Foster often went out with his father in *Snowdrop* crabbing. The boat is close to Point at high water.

A Family Group.
Fisherman George Foster sits in his half waders with his grandson George, wife Elizabeth, son Henry George and daughter in law Jenny. His daughter Henrietta (Hettie) is sitting.

George Reeve.
He is here putting a weight on his mooring for his boat. He was the caretaker of the Tilley Institute for some years.

George and Bessie Foster.
They are in their garden for this probable 1914 photograph. He was a full-time fisherman owning *Snowdrop*. He also played the organ in the Methodist church for some years.

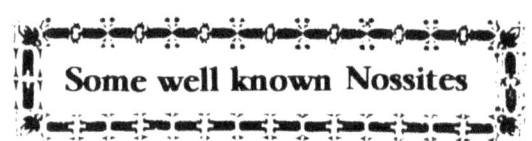
Some well known Nossites

Vince Hodge's Bake House

The bake house at No. 10 Noss is quite old. It is known that the Finch family, followed by the Rowe family, baked here for the villagers. Father Vince was educated at Noss School. In his early teens he went to London to learn banking but not liking the city life, he returned to Noss and rented the bake house from the 2nd Lord Revelstoke's estate in the early 1900s. He was assisted by his younger brother Jack until he emigrated to Canada in 1911 or 1912.

The oven is unique, being basically a hole dug in the earth bank, the arched top lined with bricks and the baking surface tiled. Hard anthracite or coke was used to heat the oven. When the bread was being baked the heat from the fire was diverted up the chimney. Dough mixing started at 4.30 a.m. to have the bread ready and steaming hot by 9 a.m. Vince and his wife were hard workers.

After the end of the 1914-18 war the son helped out. In the mid 1920s young Vince joined the Merchant Navy as a junior officer. Before too long he picked up a mysterious ailment in the tropics and started wasting away. After weeks in hospital he was allowed home still too weak to walk. Bill Finch, his school boy friend, used to collect him evenings and carry him piggy back to the Tilley Institute or to one of the village pubs. Vincent's illness lasted a long time.

He eventually started working again in the bake house which he ran after his parents had retired. Soon after the Second World War he was assisted by Bill Crook. Vince later acquired the *Swan Inn* and he died in 1957 or thereabouts. The Hodges had run the bake house for close on sixty years. Bill Finch was serving on a Navy supply ship during the last war which was torpedoed. After spending many hours in the water he was rescued but died soon afterwards through inhaling fuel oil on the water.

Father Vince lost a young son who fell over the cliff along Passage Road. There is a broken monument marking the spot. Jack Hodge, the eldest son, passed as a Dockyard apprentice. He was a keen footballer with the Yealm United team before accepting an appointment with the Admiralty at Bath. Daughters Marjorie and Ethel ran a successful beauty parlour in Plymouth before marrying and leaving Noss.

Reg Doddridge

Reg, together with his brother Len, started the first motor carrier service between Plymouth, Newton and Noss around 1926. We local boys used to love to ride in the back of the several canvas-covered Chevrolet lorries, running errands and delivering packages. For many of us this was the first motor vehicle we rode in apart from the buses.

Reg was a stocky man, always wearing a cap, collarless shirt, breeches and leggings. Summertime he wore a sleeveless waistcoat, winters he added a shapeless hat. This sturdy man could wrestle fifty gallon beer barrels with ease mounting them on trestles for the various landlords. Besides having the ability to drive a wide lorry at excessive speeds through narrow country lanes without fender bending, our friend Reg had a very good memory returning from Plymouth without the need for a shopping list. He also was blessed with a mathematical mind being able to add and multiply large numbers without the use of pencil and paper.

He was also a keen supporter of the Plymouth Argyl football team attending the games regardless of the weather. A well informed student of the third and fourth leagues he was the vocal leader announcing to the world when Argyl scored a goal. When his team faced a possibly foul Reg would not hesitate to inform the referee and his captive audience surrounding him on the terrace at Home Park, that the referee was going blind or needed crutches to keep up with the play.

Sam Axworthy

A widower, he lived alone at No. 9 Noss Mayo. Having fought in the First World War, he had a talent for collecting army uniforms preferring the ones with a tunic and breeches which he always wore with his sea boots. Sam had many occupations having an old 14 ft. boat he would take people fishing, ferry people from the *Princess Royal* and the *Princess Alexandra*, the paddle wheel excursion steamers from Plymouth and, at low tide, he often dug worms selling them at one shilling per hundred.

There were no radios in those days. Summer evenings Sam would often sit on the steps of his house entertaining anyone who would listen to his old English concertina. When he died he was found just inside his front door still in his army uniform.

Lionel Rowe

A very quiet character who enjoyed a few pints of scrumpy (a rough form of cider), he rarely spoke to anyone or started a conversation. Lionel had been a gunner in the trenches throughout the First World War ending up with a bad case of trench foot. He could never walk properly yet he was always employed as a builder's labourer earning a living mixing concrete and carrying materials in all kinds of weather. He must have suffered intensely with his feet. He never seemed to have much yet he was always cheerful.

Edwardian Dance Club in the early 1950s.

Recognised here in Noss village hall, *back row left to right*, are Daniel Shepherd, D. Davenport, Norman Doddridge, Pat Baker, Annie Cawse, Flo Pearce, Ruth Doddridge, Mrs. D. Doddridge, John and Joan Johnson, Mr. Dyer, Jack Hall, Dick Attwell. *Middle row*: Hannah Prynne, Mrs. Snelling, Elsie Browne, Vera Pearse, Phyllis Nicholson, Pat Harris, Violet Easton, Mr. Easton, *violinist*, Evelyn Holloway, Dorothy and George Bradley, Phyllis Hall, Terry Meehan, Miriam Aggett, Jack Attwell. *Front row*: Frank Rhymes, Clarence Nicholson, Mrs. Smith, Mrs. Crocker, Mrs. Toms, Iris Rhymes, Lilian Parsons, Harry Hele, *pianist*, Mrs. Crocker, Mrs. Hele, *instructress*, Mabel Dyer, Queenie Hodge, Esther Pearse, Helen and Mrs. Rowsell, Sidney Aggett, Flossie Adams, Cissy Aggett.

He obtained double value from his tobacco, chewing it before he smoked it. Lionel was a regular bell ringer chiming no. 4 bell yet he was never seen attending services.

One evening a few eyebrows were raised in the *Globe Inn* when he, on a busy summer's evening, tired of waiting at the bar for a pint of scrumpy attracted mine host, the venerable Mr. Scaddon, by addressing him as a drunkard's labourer.

The Crocker Family

Many generations of this family have lived at Noss. They were mostly stone masons and builders, their skills being passed down from father to son. Some of them helped to build St. Peter's church. Family members had many side lines. Prior to a disease decimating the local rabbit population, Jack and Fern trapped rabbits supplying the village with meat and selling their pelts. Jim Crocker did not follow the family tradition, he served in the navy and on retirement joined the customs service not following in the footsteps of an ancestor, a well known smuggler Tom Crocker.

Stan, better known as Foreman, was jack of all trades working on the buildings by day and helping out in the bar of the *Swan Inn* in the evenings. Sunday mornings he was bell ringing. Returning to his cellar at the Voss steps he held a lively conversation on the state of the world with his clients as they waited for a haircut. He cut hair with one eye closed and his head tilted to one side trying to keep the cigarette smoke of his eyes. Stan operated with hand-activated clippers. If the customer complained that they pulled he would reach for another which pulled even more. We were always glad to pass over our shilling and escape more torture.

In my youth Doris Crocker, a sweet little girl, used to sit opposite me in the Noss church choir. Doris, now Mrs. Bert Marsden, is a lovely white haired lady who still sits in the same seat. She has sung in the choir for close on fifty-five years.

Herbert and the Baker Boys

Herbert was widowed when my mother's sister Emily died. He would spend many an evening with my parents for companionship. One valentine's day a jubilant Herbert arrived waving a card saying that it came from a girl friend. My parents were always curious about this friend as they had sent the card.

Lionel, the eldest son, left the area and joined the London police soon after the end of the First World War. Bob was well known and well liked by everyone. He was outspoken and a keen sportsman playing football for Noss when he was young, swimming in the regattas, winning many races using the old fashioned side stroke. He also won many races with the greyback crews until he was fifty years of age. In the 1950s he had the 14 ft. International *San Toy* boat and won many sailing races.

Prior to the Second World War he started the Jubilee Springs furniture business as a small concern which grew to employ over ninety workers. Unfortunately the factory in Plymouth was burned down by incendiary bombs and he lost everything.

After serving in the army he restarted the business in the old Grand Theatre. He was competing with government financed utility brand of furniture and packed it in after two years. He then started making rustic bird boxes in a barn on Netton farm. After Bob died his son in law and daughter transferred the business to Membland. Bob Baker's bird boxes are still being made supplying many overseas markets.

I think it was the year 1952 when Mrs. Vincent Hodge presented the prizes at Newton. Bob had won many for rowing and sailing. At this prize giving Bob shook hands with his aunt Blanche and kissed her on her cheeks on every occasion. The crowd applauded his efforts and aunt Blanche, the stately matriarch of the Hodge family, always needed a few seconds to straighten her hat and regain her composure before the prize giving could continue.

Elliot, an excellent athlete, was troubled with asthma when he was young and for many years was mine host at the *Swan Inn* before moving to Ugborough with his wife Monica to own his own pub.

Victor, the youngest, had a personality similar to Bob. He joined the Royal Air Force as a pilot at the beginning of the war. His Hampton bomber was shot up over Germany and he just made the Kent coast where he had to bail out. Afterwards he volunteered to fly as a navigator on another bombing mission which never returned. The date was August, 1941.

Ralph Hockaday

Ralph started with his son John as an apprentice building crabbers and small boats in Hockaday's yard, located where the conveniences now stand by the playing ground. They built the crabbers *Mabel* and *Quickstep*, also the *Idle Hour* for a Mr. Shepherd, a local builder in return for repair work to their home.

Ralph joined the Devonshire Regiment in the First World War, sailed for the Persian Gulf and was involved in the very tragic Kut-el-Amara garrison siege in Iraq. The garrison held out for five months against the Turks. The siege ended in a Turkish victory on 29th April, 1916, when 13,500 men of the British Imperial army were taken prisoner. The garrison consisted of a few Russians, Indian troops and 2,592 British troops.

The prisoners faced a march of 800 miles to Baghdad and then on to Mosal where a railway was being constructed to link Instanbul in Turkey with Baghdad. The British with a few Russians were separated from the Indian troops and under the control of Turkish troopers the march began.

No boots or clothing were available. The food consisted of watery milk, rice soup and black gritty Turkish bread or flour when bread was not available with a little salt. To quote son John's writing "Father marched 200 miles in 120 degree heat and was carried the last four miles by two mates, one called Smale and the other Sherriff, both

A Maun of Bait.
The fishermen are standing close to Noss Voss with a basket or *maun* showing part of a ray hanging over its edge. This was used as bait. Harry Foster, son Sydney and George Foster, who used to preach in the chapel, make up this group behind which is a crabbing boat.

At Pope's Quay.
It is about 1925 and George Foster is about to go out in his small rowing boat to collect crabs from various pots laid the previous day. They would normally be taken to the Barbican for sale at the daily fish market.

158 PH *Snowdrop*
Three generations of Fosters. Young Georgie, sitting on the bow with her father, Henry George (Harry) and grandfather George behind.

from the Saltash area. They were put on a boat called the *Julnar* a paddle steamer operating on the river Tigris. A Turkish doctor checked them over. Ralph Hockaday was listed as an exchange prisoner, at this point weighing only 5 stone 6 lbs. The prisoners who carried him, being stronger, had to go on another forced march from which they failed to survive.

70% of the British troops died of malnutrition, cholera, malaria and dysentery. The fallen were left by the road side to rot in the sun. They also had to fight off raids by Arabs trying to steal their possessions. They had no shelter, clothing or medicines. Wounds were infected by maggots. They were often short of water, sharing water bottles.

Ralph did not start his return to England until three months after the Armistice in 1918, sailing from Port Said to Taranto in southern Italy and then by train to Calais. He was twice mentioned in dispatches and received the Military medal for his efforts in the relief of the garrison at Kut-el-Amara.

Ralph and his wife Hilda ran the post office and shop at the bottom of Pillory Hill from 1932 to 1959. He spoke with a slight lisp and is well remembered for his witty remarks and smile which often brought colour to the cheeks of the lady customers.

Stanley Paige

Farmer Stanley Paige, J.P. of Coombe Farm, was always very popular especially with the young people of the village. Stanley and son Tom farmed a very hilly area. They were great horse lovers using them to pull the ploughs and binders for several years after other farmers had turned to tractor power. One afternoon when Stanley was clearing a choked binder a horse moved. The huge needle for tying the sheaves of corn penetrated the back of the farmer's hand. He was lucky to get his hand free without it being badly mangled.

Stanley was the most generous farmer in the area in giving the youngsters the rabbits caught in the harvest fields. He took a keen interest in village life and events. For many years he started firing the guns for the Yealm regattas. Mrs. Paige ran the dairy. The morning milk was delivered. We had to bring our cans to buy the evening milk after 4.30 p.m. It is a pity that we can no longer visit the farm for that wonderful rich creamy milk.

Membland George

Membland George was a flamboyant character arriving at Noss in the earl days of the war with his clean cut appearance, swagger stick and style. He could pass as a gentleman's gentleman. He spoke with a highly cultured cockney accent and was always well dressed.

George had risked his life in rescuing the life of a wounded officer in no man's land in front of the trenches during the First World War. This ex-officer was George's employer, who having purchased a large house at Membland, took good care of him by employing him as head gardener and bottle washer.

Friday or Saturday evenings George would arrive at Noss to do his banking at the *Swan Inn*. He was the funniest humorist we had in those gloomy days. The more he invested the happier he got. George always left the *Swan* with bottles in his pockets, sometimes finding it difficult to carry them back to Membland.

Herbert Stone

It was in 1934 when Herbert Stone sailed the *Trade Winds*, a 40 ft. ex-Morecombe Bay prawner converted to a yacht with a yawl rig, into the Yealm. He suffered from polio when young and could not handle the yacht himself. Jumbo Hodge was his weekend crew. Before too long many of us "water rats" became acquainted with the old gent, delivering his mail and running errands. In return he taught us how to read the weather, the basics of coastal navigation, often taking about a dozen of us sailing in fine weather.

Herbert used to smoke a formidable pipe keeping his tobacco in a jar lodged on a shelf under the cabin table. One Sunday, finding a thermos flask rolling around the cabin, I placed it in the tobacco jar. Later, needing some coffee, I found that the flask had broken and we rolled the coffee-tobacco mix in newspapers to dry it out. We were afraid to ask Herbert if he liked his new brand of tobacco.

Herbert, a good friend to many of us, lies buried in Noss churchyard. The *Trade Winds* dragged her moorings in a gale and she was broken up.

Jim and Ivor Parsons

Jim and Ivor were brothers who for many years worked the old blacksmith's forge on the hill leading to Bridgend. They were busy working on farm machinery and shoeing horses. Jim was the expert horse shoer. After the hot shoe was taken from the forge to be fitted to the horse's hoof and the smoke rose, horses often became frightened and troublesome. Jim used words which only the horse understood and obeyed.

Ivor was the head bell ringer at Revelstoke for many years often winning bell ringing contests. The church hand bells were taken to the village at Christmas time the ringing usually started at the *Swan Inn*. The bells are held by straps and are rung by flicking the wrist and stopping the bell with the thumb at the correct moment. Most bell ringers played the peals thinking they were great.

Ivor would stand in front of the ringers and where he pointed the bell was rung. He had an amazing ability to play carols by this method. The old forge closed when the brothers obtained work in Devonport dockyard.

George Hodge, Junior

My uncle, George Hodge, Jr., the skipper's eldest son, was a very well known Noss character. He ran the ferries from Steer Point meeting the trains soon after they started in 1898 until they first stopped running in 1930.

He was a good looking husky man, six feet tall, always taking a great pride in his appearance. He grew a long moustache in his youth which his mother disliked. One evening when George was asleep Grandma Hodge, assisted by mother holding a candle, cut off one half of his precious face piece with a snip of the scissors. This painless snipping operation was a sore point for many days. After the *Kitley Belle* stopped running George went poultry farming in Cornwall returning to work on the Plymouth tug boats at the outbreak of the war.

In his old age he did not have much to look forward to but he had a marvelous memory and liked to talk about the past. He would have been of great assistance in writing this book. Much to his wife's distress his many nephews made sure the George never suffered from a dry throat; we enjoyed hearing his stories.

Harold Sims

In the 1930s there were two families named Sims living at Noss. They were unrelated. Harold Sims, a small likeable man, had fished all his working life. He was a keen sportsman taking an interest in the local football team and the regattas.

When the 14 ft. Internationals were popular on the Yealm, it was always Noss against Newton with each village having two very fast dinghies. Sailing the Yealm can be compared to a game of chess. One had to tack in the right place at the right time to gain an advantage from the strong tides and gusty winds. In the post mortems after the races Harold could explain the mistakes. He had certainly mastered the art of sailing on the Yealm.

were basically lorries with four lines of seats across with a canvas top and side screens which were seldom fitted. The first was a failure, being too heavily built for the steep hills, the second was lighter and a little better. After a couple of years they were sold to the Devon Motor Transport Co., the forerunner of the Western National line.

In 1929 the Great Western Railway started a bus service meeting the trains at Yealmpton for Noss. In 1930 the trains stopped running and buses to Plymouth took over.

The *Kitley Belle* was moored off Wide Slip until 1933 when she was sold for £75 to the Millbrook Steamboat Co. who fitted her with a steering shelter and a new Gardener 6L2 diesel engine. For many years she ran the Millbrook to Mutton Cove, Devonport, ferry service and often took passengers to Cargreen and Calstock up the Tamar. She was commandeered by the Navy in 1940 and was used extensively in the Sound. At the end of the war she was sold to someone in Southhampton. Nothing more is known of her.

The *Pioneer* hung around the Yealm for many years. She was never given the engine she needed. Elliot Hodge broke her up in 1946, a good vessel wasted.

The skipper, George John Elliot Hodge died at the age of 78 in January, 1926. Apart from visits to Plymouth the furthest he ventured was one train journey to Southampton.

Saturday Patrons at the *Swan Inn* about 1949.
Left to *right:* Bill Thompson, Bill Roach with cap, the local ferryman, Norman Williams, Unknown, Bill Furzeland, Dick Rowsell drinking, Bob Andrews with hands in pockets, Owen Rowsell, Father Dick Rowsell, short with trilby hat, Two unknowns, Don Marquis smoking a pipe, Vincent Hodge landlord of the *Swan Inn*, George Bradley with shaved head, Two unknowns, Hartley Townsend with cap, Unknown and Archie Tope on the far right.

Bob Scaddon

The Globe always fascinated me as when very young. I listened to Grandma Hodge's tales of smugglers, some of which were true. During Mr. McIver's time we never went the inn. It was about 1934 when Bob Scaddon and his family moved into the inn. I did not become a customer until the last months of the war. Mrs. Scaddon, a very pleasant woman, never assisted in the bar. Bob worked there seven days a week often helped by his daughter Marie, a school mistress, and Jack, the son, an electrician.

Bob Scaddon was the only landlord that I have met who really knows how to mature beer. He would never sell a glass unless the brew was in perfect condition. The glasses were always spotless and clean tea cloths covered every barrel. Bob was always pleasant but rarely entered into conversation.

For many years the same crowd patronised the small room at Sunday lunch time. They were Elliot Hodge, a boat builder, later to be the first river Yealm harbour master. Bob Baker, a furniture manufacturer, an absolute master of his trade and understanding woods from all over the world. Cliff Parsons, a retired farmer who still got up early mornings to fish in his black and white 14 ft. boat. His knowledge of horses and farming made interesting conversation. Harold Sims, whose crabber the *Eagle* was now derelict. He had a 14 ft. boat with a Seagull outboard for crabbing. His main interest was the local sailing races. Arthur Hamm, in the motor industry, later to marry Marie, the landlord's daughter. She often joined us at the table enjoying the conversations.

We did not drink much but were all good friends with different occupations and interests. As soon as Bob Scaddon retired we drifted apart as the bar was modernised and the place changed. We missed the old world atmosphere and the golden brew was not carbonated. We did not appreciate the new furnishings and the change of name to *The Olde Ship*.

Sarah Elliot

She lived at Globe Cottage and used to make and sell her home brew in the days before the carriers connected Noss with Plymouth. She married Uncle Joe Penwell who lived in the *Old Ship* building. This was originally a wine storage cellar with accommodation over it. Sarah used to sell her brew from this cellar area. Uncle Joe was a fisheman who did a little smuggling to keep up the stock of wines.

My grandmother, Mary Jane Pope, who lost her mother when she was six years of age was brought up by the Penwells. In 1850 she married George Elliot Hodge, a fisherman, who lived in the house on the beach below Globe Cottage to the south of the *Old Ship Inn*. This marriage produced twelve children the family living in various Globe houses until 1887 when Uncle Joe died and they then moved to No. 50 Noss Mayo across the creek.

Rev. L. A. W. Woolcombe

The Rev. Woolcombe moved into the parish in 1928 living with his mother and sister Joy, staying until 1935. He was always an ailing man having been gassed in the First World War, yet he did more for the villagers than any other vicar except perhaps Rev. W. E. Roome, M.A., the vicar who taught at Noss school from 1890 to 1922.

The rectory opened up for the villagers. There was maypole dancing, sporting events and tea parties in an endeavour to raise money for the preservation of old Stoke church and other causes. Assisted by his sister Joy, Johnny Wakeham's two daughters from Rowden farm (I remember one as Mary) with Mr. Ching from Newton Ferrers and others, troops of Brownies, Girl Guides and Boy Scouts were formed. Evenings spent at the rectory were very important in our young lives, learning to tie knots, about nature and the outdoors.

The troop of Scouts attended a world jamboree held at Birmingham the first time many had ever left the village. The vicar produced several popular well attended nativity plays at St. Peters. It was a great loss when the church re-allocated him away from here. After a few months the scouting folded up.

Rev. R. I. F. Garrod 1935-46

The next vicar was a refined quiet and older man. He did not have the charisma and following of his predecessor. He is remembered for his passionate sermons, waving his arms, often breaking the pulpit in his endeavors. Mrs. Brittain, a Londoner, lived at Noss during the war years and often sang solos in the choir attracting the congregation on Sunday mornings. Few people knew that she was Olive Tyson the famous opera singer.

Rev. G. R. Channer 1947-61

The Rev. Channer was a good vicar and a broad minded person. He did not hide in the vicarage but lived in the village visiting people in their homes; he was very generous in gifts to the sick and elderly.

In the late 1950s when Elliot and Monica Baker hosted the *Swan* tables were laid out and after the harvest festival service the fruit and produce were taken to the inn. Another service was held and Elliot auctioned off the produce raising record sums of money for church charities. This was really bringing the church to the people who normally never attended.

Miss Minnie Lancaster

My mother, farmer Dick Chaffe and George Foster, lifetime friends, often spoke highly of the Rev. Roome who had taught then at Noss School. I believe the next teacher was Miss Minnie Lancaster who lived at No. 51 Noss. She was assisted by Miss Chandler, the infant teacher, in the small room of the school. For many years these ladies taught an average of fifty pupils in a class.

Captain Robert Hodge Mashford and his Family.
This wonderful family group photograph dates from 1893 outside of Ferry Cottage. His wife Jane (Avery from Wembury) is with their children these being Mathias Darton, Sidney Edward Darton, William George Darton, Violet Mary Darton, Frank Darton, Frederick Darton, Mabe Eva Darton, Rose Jane Darton and Emily Darton.

Yealm United Football Team Club 1919-20
E. Gill, C. Lake, P. Hockaday, E. Blackmore, F. Lake, W. Staplehurst, Mr. V. Hodge, president, F. Roseveare, A. Roach, S. Roach, J. Hisbent, captain, H. Squire, F. Land, secretary and treasurer, N. Bunker, E. Richards, E. Shepherd, N. Wyatt, H. Kingcombe, J. Axworthy, J. Hodge, W. Tope and R. Kingcombe.

Minnie, a strict disciplinarian, was a great believer in her theory that learning had to be assisted by canning. The education given was very good, the majority of pupils passing the scholarships to gain higher education at Plympton grammar school. Minnie gave the school a lot of her private time in teaching the youngsters to swim after school. She was always burdened walking home with exercise books to be corrected.

Minnie and Miss Chandler, assisted by Mrs. Rowsell on the piano, put on excellent school Christmas concerts for many years. It was about 1936 when Minnie Lancaster was moved to be head teacher at Newton school. Miss Chandler stayed at Noss.

Mrs. Fenton

Mrs Fenton was the next to the last head mistress at Noss school living with her husband and three daughters in a house in the field at Hannaford.

She was a quiet person taking a great interest in botany. She was an expert pianist and was very popular. Half the school, although uninvited, would follow her to the beach. She stayed until Noss school closed soon after the end of the 1939-45 war.

Miss Chandler

She was the infant teacher at Noss school for more years than I can remember. Before the war there were not any nursery schools many children starting when a little over four years old. She had the necessary patience and ability to take good care and teach the little piddlers. She taught many hundreds of them and they all loved her.

Miss Chandler lodged with Mr. E. M. Mashford behind the Tilley Institute; she was a very private person who faded into the scenario. When she became ill she quietly left the village to die of cancer in a Plymouth hospital.

Emily and Jack Mashford

Emily and her sister, Jane, lived on small pensions in a house having a large garden behind the Tilley Institute. To supplement their income they grew flowers which were in great demand to take to the churchyard Saturday evenings. It was considered a disgrace at that time not to have fresh flowers on a grave prior to Sunday morning service. They also made several varieties of jam which they sold.

These two church going ladies were first class wine makers, making raspberry, loganberry, rhubarb, parsnip and ginger wines. They were very much in demand for Christmas.

Christmas, while growing up in Noss, is fondly remembered. There were eight of my mother's sisters and brothers living in the village. At Christmas evening family members congregated to visit Grandma Hodge at No. 50. The presents were laid out on a circular table in the front room. I remember that one of my gifts was a clockwork motor car.

A party was going on in the stone flagged kitchen with quite a lot of singing and laughter. As on every Christmas there were several gallons of E. M. Mashford's wine, glasses being topped up frequently by the inebriated who tried to make the more sober members of the family join their happy ranks.

We grand children were sent into the front room to enjoy ourselves. We acquired a bottle of wine which passed from mouth to mouth and we became a little high on this tonic water. Roger was alarmed to see the flames in the fireplace reaching as high as the mantelpiece. There was no street lighting in those days so this little boy, who still believed in Father Christmas, fairies, elves and bogey men, was sent to look for the fire engine up Pillory Hill. Breathlessly he returned not able to find it but to find at least five of his cousins with their little hoses in hand trying to subdue the flames with the young female family members looking on in amazement.

The Revels

Clump Revel was the local carrier for many years often assisted by his son Bert. They lived at No. 40 Noss. Their vehicle was on old heavy two-wheeled cart which had seen better days. It was pulled by an old horse which always traveled at a slow speed. Clump and his ancient rig were often seen going along the foreshore between Noss and Newton, this route bypassing the hills.

He used to sit sideways on the cart shafts holding the reins. This pair would move anything that was not nailed down. One day the horse shied on Back Road near the church and Clump received a head injury from which he never recovered. Reg Dodderidge, the Plymouth carrier, purchased the a pair of boots for Bert. Next day Bert was seen sitting on a wall by his steps wearing heavy socks and soaking his boots in a pan of water. He explained that he walked until the boots were dry and they then fitted his feet perfectly.

As soon as Bert received his old age pension he put aside his working clothes and changed into a country gentleman wearing breeches, polished brown boots and leather leggings, shirt with collar and tie, tweed coat and felt hat. He spent his days walking around the village accompanied by his brown and white spaniel dog. If one in greeting Bert passed the time of day he would stop in his stride, turn around and look at the person with his one eye and say "Ow be e boy?" even if the person he was addressing was a lady.

He had a problem carrying scrumpy with decorum, at times becoming a little obstreperous. He was banned from the pubs after he threw one of Elliot's pint mugs through a window at the *Swan Inn*. He was a regular scrounger and would offer a stranger a penny to buy a cigarette, hoping to get the whole packet.

Bert was given custody of his sister's black and white cat while she was away. He had other ideas. He put the cat in a sack with a stone, walked down Passage Road intending to drown it when Cordelia Axworthy, a local beauty, heard the cries from the sack and liberated it. Bert, the one eyed pirate, was no match for the infuriated Cordy now armed with a stone in the sack. He made a hasty retreat to the village.

Vince and Blanche outside their bakery, Noss.
Vince employed Edith Javelin to deliver bread and cakes
in a van and Bill Crocker worked with them for some years.
Sunday dinners could be cooked in their oven, ginger and
fruit cakes and scones were made. Vince started work at 4 a.m.

William John Hockaday

Presentation at the Edwardian Dancing Club.
Miriam Aggett is making a presentation to Harry Hele, the
pianist, in about 1950 in Noss village hall. Recognised are
John Stitson, Edith Spiller, Jack Hall and Hedley Spiller.
Theses dances lasted for about six years and were very popular
among the village people.

Bill Roach

He was a naval pensioner who lived alone in a flat over what was then a cellar by the Newton Voss steps. Close to forty years Bill ran the very important ferry services between Newton and Noss carrying annually hundreds of passengers. Regardless of the weather, summer and winter, he was always obliging yet when rowing the river he grumbled all the way across to his passengers.

Bill loved his whisky with a beer chaser. He did his banking at the *Globe, Swan* or *Dolphin Inns*. When we were kids we used to nip in with our old leaky "Tom Tit" and steal a few of his fares. Eventually he would corner the crew of the opposing ferry, glare at us for a while, then take his pipe from his mouth and blast off at us using all the descriptive words learnt in the navy. For quite awhile he addressed me as "young bastard". One cold morning Bill was found dead fully dressed in his bed. His old walking stick and photo are in the *Dolphon Inn*.

Harry Williams

Old Harry, as we called him, arrived at Noss just before the Second World War. He appeared to be a loner never talking about himself. I got to know him slightly by giving him a lift from Brixton to Noss on my way home from work in Plymouth. As the years passed Harry got older and frailer. Always in his fawn raincoat he kept busy by doing odd jobs around the village. For several years he pumped the organ at St. Peters starting at 17s 6d which was eventually raised to the princely sum of 22s 6d for a thirteen week quarter. The church goers ignored his plight.

When poor Harry was broke and homeless, not wanting to leave Noss, Bob baker and his wife made over and furnished a shed at the top of their garden for him. Bob and his wife Gladys took good care of him for a long time before he was unable to care for himself and he then had to go into a nursing home.

John Sims

A big man with a goatee beard, he had been the electrician at Membland. He lived at Point House with his petite wife Emma. He fished with Dick Light in a crabber and for a learner he did reasonably well. The established local fishermen netted a large school of mullet in Noss Creek and the net was hauled on to the foreshore on Point side. John wanted a share in the catch although he was not a shareholder in it. Blows were exchanged which were never forgotten by the fishermen in the village, John's fishing days were over.

When the wealthier Foxworthy family moved into Battery Cottage, John with his son Henry, who had been wounded and invalided out of the navy, obtained the positions of chauffeur, boatmen and general helpers. They were instrumental in hanging the barbed wire which fenced off the Battery area. At one time the path to Cellars Beach was also wired off.

John had another son Hubert, nick named Poop by the villagers, who was in the police living in London. Neither sons married. The parents sold Point House and built another one at the top of Back Road near the church. On retiring Hubert walked the village daily rarely speaking to anyone, still wearing his police boots. Henry rarely left the house, village boys used to torment him. He could not tolerate whistling. Yet when the spirit moved him he would visit the church belfry on Sunday afternoons chiming out popular hymns on the bells.

The two brothers were not compatible. It is possible that Henry, who died first, did not leave a will. After Hubert's death the interior of the house was found to be wrecked with holes in the walls and floor boards ripped up. Hubert had been looking for money which Henry was supposed to have hidden in the house.

George Reeves

He was for many years the caretaker of the Tilley Institute, a typical Noss character set in his ways. Never without his soft cloth cap, collarless shirt with a stud in the top hole, trousers supported by braces assisted by a wide leather belt with a heavy brass buckle. In the warm weather he wore his waistcoat unbuttoned, in cold weather buttoned. He was never without a yellowed skinny hand-rolled cigarette.

He kept the billiard tables spotless, always in first class condition. Youngsters under the age of sixteen were not admitted to his hallowed domain. George would not tolerate any skylarking whatsoever. His hobbies were billiards and snooker, a little gardening and fishing in his 14 ft. rowing boat, usually alone. George was a pleasant serious person, we never saw him enjoy a good laugh.

One 5th November we had him really upset for about an hour. A string was attached to the clanger on the school bell. George never learnt that the phantom bell ringer was Jack Shepherd, the present caretaker of the institute, standing alongside him.

Bill Hall

He was the sexton at the church for over thirty-five years living with his family above Lord Revelstoke's coach stables facing the church. Bill did an excellent job in keeping the church clean and the churchyard mowed and tidy.

He saw the happy times at christenings and weddings as well as the sorrowing at the grave sides all of which is village life. After he passed on his daughter Patsy with her husband, Raymond Martin, took excellent care of the church properties for nineteen years.

Populations and Public Houses

The Devonshire Calendar and Register by Percy, 1876, states:
- Revelstoke parish registration dates from 1654
- Holbeton parish registration dates from 1620
- Newton Ferrers parish registration dates from 1600
- Population at Noss in 1841 was 603
- Population at Noss in 1861 was 505
- Population at Noss in 1871 was 464 (215 males)

The *Swan Inn* and *The Olde Ship (Globe)* date back before 1850 when trade directories were first published. In 1871 there was a *Union Inn* at Noss and a *Victoria Inn* at Bridgend.

It is believed that the *Union Inn* was run by Sarah Elliot. It was an ale house selling porter, mead and ale, no beer. It was where No. 26 Noss Mayo now stands. These two houses probably sold home brew made from local grain dried at the Malt House. The *Victoria Inn* was at the back of the Malt House at Bridgend close by the small stream which passes under the road.

The *Swan* and *Globe Inns* in the early 1900s.

The Nicholsons

Clarry was a sergeant instructor at Membland during the First World War. He married Winifred, skipper Hodge's youngest daughter. After living for a few years at Saltash they returned to Noss. They purchased two and a half acres of land from farmer Paige, cleared most of it and working together they built five 60 ft. greenhouses.

Their only piece of machinery was a 4 hp roto-tiller. The couple helped feed the village for many years with all kinds of vegetables, including tomatoes and cucumbers. Noss would have been in poor shape had it not been for this couple during the war years. After a bomb shattered the glasshouses they worked making repairs. Win had a heart attack and died in July, 1944. Besides feeding the villagers they were great entertainers both being pianists and they helped to produce many lovely concerts.

Clarry was one of the sponsors of the Edwardian dancing classes which took place in the village after 1945. Their only son, Jack, stayed in the R.A.F. after the war, traveled the world and ended his career as a Squadron Leader. He is now a talented local artist. With an average of over 500 inhabitants living in Noss it is impossible to write about all the characters. Most now lie as silent memories in the church yard.

The servicemen engaged in the two world wars are remembered on the plaques at the back of the church. The memorial to the fallen is in the church yard. For many years Ralph Hockaday recited the eulogy at the Armistice services. Clarence Hodge, a very popular Noss resident and close friend is the only war casualty interred at Noss. Clarence (Jumbo) aged 26, in the Merchant Navy, was helping to save a stricken tanker off Portland Bill when he was hit in the spine by machine gun bullets from a German aircraft.

Roger Aggett

Roger still remembers the thrashing his mother gave him for taking his younger brother, Alan, down the Voss steps from No. 50 to that wonderful forbidden Foster's cellar and painting his brother's hands and face with tar which his tearful mother removed with melted butter. This happy little boy, always shoe deep in mud, considered schooling a waste of time. Every school report said that he could do better, a cruel report for this little genius who could swim, handle boats, catch fish and sail at a very early age. He always tilled the garden, getting into trouble for planting beans in the flower garden.

Barely sixteen years of age Roger started as a boat building apprentice building his first 27 ft. naval lifeboat after twenty months. He was promoted to a foreman when he finished his six year apprenticeship. He worked throughout the war on new constructions for the Navy and the R.A.F. In 1946 his company opened a branch at Salcombe making him its manager. In 1951 he started his own company where he designed and built close to a hundred boats and yachts, twenty-eight being sold in the U.S.A. In 1961 the rented workshop was auctioned at a price Roger could not afford. Consequently he had to seek other employment. In 1963 Luders Marine Construction Co., of Stamford, Connecticut, sought his services and while there he helped build two of the America's Cup defenders. Also the 5.5 meter yacht which won a Gold Cup in the Olympic Games. In 1964 Mr. Luders died and the following year the yard closed.

Roger putting his tool box and all his worldly goods in his Pontiac drove south for four days stopping at Daytona Beach. He was soon made foreman in new construction and production manager within five years. This yard employed an average of seventy-five craftsmen custom building powerful fast sports fishermen from 41 ft. to 65 ft. long. The yard also handled all types of repairs on vessels up to 150 ft.

In July, 1974, the yard was sold to a financier who knew very little about the industry or the skills involved. After two weeks Roger gave one month's notice and left.

He then studied and obtained a coast guard captain's licence to operate his private diesel sports fishermen in the charter business. In the meanwhile he was studying to pass the examination set by the National Association of Marine Surveyors. He received certification to professionally survey vessels up to 100 net tons. Roger Aggett., Inc. was then formed. Surveys took him to England, Canada, the eastern seaboard of the U.S. and many islands in the Caribbean. He retired after 19 years surveying and being an expert court witness in 1993. Roger was busy designing, building and racing fibre glass radio-controlled yachts in the 36/600 class before retiring to Noss in 1999.

Grandma Hodge, wife of George, *Kitley Belle* skipper.

John Rowsell and Roger Aggett in 1994.

Lifeboats on the River Yealm

The English Channel has always been a busy highway for vessels both large and small many floundering or being washed ashore with loss of life. The first lifeboat was presented to Plymouth by Mr. Phillip Longmead, a local Member of Parliament, in 1803. Nothing is known about this boat except that she was the forerunner of many lifeboats to appear in the south-western waters of the channel.

On the 14th February, 1874, the small steamer *Aivali* of Marseilles was driven ashore in a storm on the coastline of Mothercombe. The crew of nine were saved by the Mothercombe coastguard. Chief boatman, Edwin Parker, was awarded a silver medal by the R.N.L.I. This rescue received much publicity. The local residents asked the R.N.L.I. to open a station in the district. A meeting was held on 1st March, 1877, and it was decided to open one on the Yealm river, there being sufficient numbers of fishermen available to make up a crew.

The Rev. Duke Young, vicar of Holy Cross, donated the land. The house and slipway were built below where the Yealm Hotel now stands. The first lifeboat to be allocated to the new station was the *Bowman*. This was a new vessel, self-righting, of the rowing-sailing type, weighing 3,110 lbs., rowed by ten men with a full crew of thirteen. She cost £433 to build being given by an anonymous donor having the initials A.B.S. The crew consisted of Newton men, the coxswain was William Hockaday. The year was 1878.

She was replaced by a more stable and modern vessel the *Daring* in 1887, donated by Mrs. Thomas of Somerset. She was a foot shorter than the previous boat but very similar costing £392 to build. In 1904 the 35 ft. x 8 ft. 0 ins. beam, self-righting, rowing-sailing vessel *Michael Smart* cost £800 to build, a legacy from Mr. M. Smart. The coxswain was a **William Hockaday.**

These lifeboats, all weighing close to one and a half tons, had to be rowed by ten oarsmen about a mile before the sails could be set and was, therefore, slow in getting to a vessel in distress. The Yealm station being quiet and not having a rescue since 1918 was closed in 1927.

The service record for the Yealm river lifeboat stationed at the western end of Bigbury Bay is:

Bowman: 28th January, 1885, barque *Wellington* of Windsor, Nova Scotia, assisted Plymouth lifeboat to save the vessel and fifteen lives.

Michael Smart: 6th August, 1904, barge *Thrush* of Plymouth saved vessel.

29th August, 1909, open boat of Plymouth, landed three persons.

21st November, 1914, steamship *Veghtstroom* of Amsterdam, stood by.

Total number of lives saved or assisted to save 1878-1927 was seventeen.

Brothers Freeman Lifeboat, 1922 to 1926.
This was the last of the sailing-rowing lifeboats stationed at Plymouth and was identical in design to the Yealm lifeboats. It is thought that this photograph was taken on her last day of service.

Hope Cove Lifeboat

Bigbury Bay to the east of the Yealm is almost eight miles across due to the shape of the coastline. Sailing vessels were often driven into the bay, many having poor windward ability when reefed in strong winds, and were driven ashore. Because of this a new lifeboat station was opened at Hope Cove. This operated for the same period as the Yealm station. Its service record is:

Alexandra 1: 18th January, 1877, ship *Halloween* of London saved nineteen lives.
Alexandra 2: 1st December, 1896, steam tanker *Blesk* of Odessa saved forty-three lives.
Alexandra 4: 25th March, 1912, schooner *Sidney Smith* of Carnarvon saved two lives.

Total number of lives saved 1874-1930 was sixty-four.

The two stations with the slow rowing-sailing lifeboats were closed because in 1926 the Plymouth station received the *Robert and Marcella Beck* which was 60 ft. long, powered by two 76 hp engines capable of nine and a half knots.

After the Yealm station was closed the lifeboat house was converted into a dwelling and the lifeboat sold to the Foxworthys for £72 10s who lived in Battery Cottage. All the sails were removed, the mast left standing, she was fitted with an engine. The outside of the hull was painted black and the raised fore and aft decks white. She was renamed the *Dominica*. A few months before the Second World War she was purchased by Elliot Hodge of Noss Mayo who intended to use her for passenger trips. However, soon after war was declared she was commandeered by the Royal Navy and ended her days on the rocks in the Portland Bill area.

The *Brothers Freeman* was the last of the Plymouth sailing and rowing lifeboats. She was an identical sister vessel to the *Michael Smart* the last R.N.L.I. lifeboat to be stationed on the Yealm. Both vessels were built by the Thames Iron Works at Blackwall, London, each costing £800.

Hope Cove lifeboat station.

Present day Yealm lifeboat house.

The *Michael Stewart* R.N.L.I. lifeboat stationed at the Yealm, 1904-27, slides down into the water from its boat house. The photograph probably records a demonstration launch in the 1910s.

Royal National Lifeboat Institution,
22 Charing Cross Road, London WC2   26th May, 1927.

Dear Sirs,
                    Yealm River Lifeboat House.

I have received a letter from the Board of Trade from which it would appear the Mr. Foxworthy's visit was attended with some success.

    It is probable that he was informed of the nature of the restrictive covenants which I do not presume are very onerous and I hope that he is now in a position to make a firm bid for the premises.

    In view of the offer of £225 which you received recently, it is hoped that Mr. Foxworthy will be prepared to pay the Institution a sum in the neighbourhood of £175 or £200. I shall be glad to hear from you again in due course when you have had an opportunity of taking your client's instructions.

                                Yours faithfully,
                                Deputy Secretary.

To: Viney, Carew and Co.,
    Prudential Buildings,

Copy of a letter from the R.N.L.I. to H. W. Foxworthy's agents in Plymouth about the sale of the lifeboat house. Mr. Foxworthy was in residence at Hillcot, Salcombe, Devon.

Patrons, Their Majesties The King & Queen

ROYAL NATIONAL LIFE BOAT INSTITUTION
for the
Preservation of Life from Shipwreck
(INCORPORATED BY ROYAL CHARTER.)
ESTABLISHED 1824.
SUPPORTED BY VOLUNTARY CONTRIBUTIONS.

PRESIDENT.
His Royal Highness the Prince of Wales, K.G.

Chairman. Sir Godfrey Baring, Bt.   Deputy Chairman. The Hon. George Colville.

CERTIFICATE OF SERVICE.

At a Meeting of the Committee of Management of the Royal National Life Boat Institution for the Preservation of Life from Shipwreck, held at their Offices, London, on the 17th day of March 1927 the following Minute was ordered to be recorded on the Books of the Society.

Resolved,

That the thanks of the Royal National Life Boat Institution be presented to Henry Hockaday on his retiring from the post of Coxswain of the Yealm River Life Boat, which he is hereby certified to have held for 28½ years, during which period he performed his duties to the entire satisfaction of the Committee.

George F. Shee, Secretary

Godfrey Baring, Chairman

Some Shipwrecks

Mariposa: Like other boys in the village we had to do our daily chores before we were allowed to enjoy ourselves. We had to fetch the bread from Hodge's bakery and the milk from farmer Paige's dairy. Summer school holidays were spent in the harvest fields following the binder, chasing rabbits, fishing off the rocks and picnicing at Old Cellars and Warren beaches. If we stayed at home we usually got trapped into weeding or gardening.

It was late August in 1930 when I was fetching the bread from Hodge's shop when I heard there was a shipwreck off the mouth of the Yealm. Returning home with the bread my brother and I and several other village boys started running down Passage Road. Stopping for breath at Battery Cottage we saw the wreck.

The *Mariposa*, having no engine, had taken advantage of the outgoing tide on a still foggy morning, had wandered off course, and grounded on the outside rock of a reef of small rocks under the headland known as Mouthstone Ledge.

Breathlessly we half skidded and half ran down the slope between the prickly gorse bushes until we came to the edge of the cliff. We had to go toward Silver Sands before finding a way to the rocks below and to get close to the wreck.

She was an old type gaff cutter about 40 ft. long with a straight stern and bowsprit, the hull painted black with a red bottom and long counter stern. She was grounded on the shore side of the outer rock held partially upright due to the shape of the rock. Her bowsprit pointed towards the Mewstone with the top of the mast leaning towards Wembury.

Elliot Hodge, later to become Yealm's first harbour master, apparently was the salvage master circling around the vessel in a rowing boat towed by his son Clarence, his 20 ft. white launch being moored further in towards Old Cellars. By afternoon many people were seated on the grass at the edge of the Drive or who had scrambled down to the cliffs. About thirty people had climb down to the rocks below. By that time farmer Chaffe and his son Roy had arrived from Worsewell farm carrying a coil of rope, obviously anxious to help.

Sometime in the afternoon a rope was rowed ashore, the other end tied to the stricken vessel. A light afternoon breeze raised swells about 18 inches high. The vessel began to right herself with Roy on board bailing furiously with a bucket. At last an order came to pull on the rope. At first attempt the rope broke and a heap of bodies had to sort themselves on the rocks below. The rope was knotted and on the next pull the *Mariposa* slid off the rocks into a gully. She was towed into the Yealm on the incoming tide and moored in the Kitley river opposite the Yealm Hotel.

The first job was to try to stop the leaking by stuffing rags in the open seams. The owner's possessions were brought ashore in the vessel's dinghy, covered with a sail and moored on the beach by Wally Austen's lifeboat house. At 7 that evening with most of the leaks stopped George Hodge, Elliot's elder brother, went on board to keep her dry, bailing a bucket of water every two or three minutes.

When Elliot arrived about 5 the next morning, George gave him a hostile welcome, the leaking had increased and he had to bail continuously to keep from swimming. Early next morning Syd Mashford from Cremyll arrived to survey the loss. He said that she was too old and strained to be worth repairing. That evening the *Mariposa* was towed up Noss creek and berthed alongside the wall of the *Globe Inn*.

The tide ran in and out of her open seams for about a week then was given to the village and broken up. Within a short time she was gone. All that remained was the heavy iron keel which lay on the beach for many years.

The next wreck occurred on a late September night just before the Second World War, 1939-45. It was blowing hard from the south-west when a yacht from Plymouth, crewed by a master and students, grounded hard on the Bar. The waves and incoming tide swept her off the Bar and drove her ashore in a cove close to Red Hole. The master and crew managed to climb up the cliffs to safety.

I did not see the wreck until the following weekend. I remember that the topsides were painted a dark cream with a red bottom. The port bilge was stoved in with planking leaving the frames. She soon broke up and disappeared with the wood either being washed or taken away.

On 8th December, 1891, the brigantine *St. Pierre* of Harve loaded with a cargo of coal briquettes experienced a storm which blew her off course, also blowing away her sails. The following day she grounded on the Mewstone rocks. The ship's boat was launched. The mate with two crew members rowed ashore for help. Meanwhile four crew members swam ashore the remaining five clung to the rigging to be rescued by the coast guard cutter.

On 6th August, 1904, the Yealm lifeboat *Michael Smart* was launched. The lifeboat located the sailing barge *Thrush* of Plymouth. The weather was rough, the barge was taking in water, she had lost her rudder and main anchor. She was moored by two makeshift anchors, was dangerously near the rocks and two crew members were exhausted by the pumping.

The crew were saved by the *Michael Smart*, the fate of the barge is not known.

Ship blown on to Wembury Rocks in 1895.
August Smith, a Norwegian 1,500 ton barque, was carrying a cargo of logwood when she was caught in a furious gale in Wembury Bay. She was driven ashore on 18th November, 1895, by a strong south-westerly gale on her route from Buenos Ayres to Rotterdam. All the crew were saved but the vessel was a total wreck.

A Yachting Mishap

Capsized Boat Taken in Tow

"ONLY A SMALL INCIDENT"

A YACHTING mishap on the River Yealm was responsible for the launching of the Plymouth lifeboat last evening.

A race was in progress under the auspices of the River Yealm Sailing Club when the leader of the five competitors, Chota, a 14-foot sailing boat, sailed by Mr. Taylor and an R.A.F. friend, capsized in rough water near Gara Point, outside the mouth of the river.

The two yachtsmen, thrown into the water, had to swim for it, but Daphne, which was following Chota in the race, soon reached the scene and within twenty minutes Mr. Taylor and his companion were "fished out," dripping but not much the worse for their experience.

Drifting Boat

Soon afterwards Dr. Stamp of Newton Ferrers in his motor boat got alongside the upturned Chota and attempted to get her in tow, but had to abandon her owing to the rough sea, and she began to drift in the direction of Mewstone Ridge.

There she might have been wrecked but for the intervention of a local boatman, Mr. E. R. Carter, who, accompanied by Mr. Leonard Modley, son of ex-Ald. W. J. W. Modley, went to the rescue in a motor launch and got the Chota in tow when she was nearing the rocks.

The Lifeboat Arrives

Mr. Carter told a "Western Independent" reporter last night that they were about half a mile away from the Ridge when the Plymouth Lifeboat arrived to give a hand.

"We were very glad of her help because, although we had the sailing boat towing behind, it was tough going and we were making only about one knot," said Mr. Carter. "The lifeboat threw a line aboard my boat and helped us back to the landing stage under the Yealm Hotel."

The Chota escaped with little damage beyond a broken mast and the loss of her rudder.

Rescuer's Comment

The Daphne, which rescued the two yachtsmen, was sailed by Mr. B. G. Gilbert, of Yealm Road, Newton Ferrers, who said last night "It was only a small incident, and nothing to make a fuss about."

The lifeboat, which was called at 5.10 and was away at 5.35, returned to her moorings at 8.20.

The River Yealm Sailing Club was formed last year.

Yachting incident near Gara Point in May, 1947.
This local report records one of the many rescues that have taken place in and around the Yealm estuary. The majority of the incidents involved small boats crewed by enthusiastic amateur yachtsmen out for a weekend's sailing when the weather takes a turn for the worse. More often than not the yachts sustain some damage but fortunately there is normally no loss of life although injuries and shock occur from time to time.

River Yealm Regattas

As no records have been kept it is possible that the first Yealm regatta started over 200 years ago. In the days of the sailing-fishing fleets there was always keen competition among the fishermen as to who possessed the fastest boats.

My mother said that there were great rowing duels between her father, skipper George Hodge, Sr., born in 1848 and members of the Rowe, Hockaday and Foster families in Noss.

There were three separate regattas held on the river, the Bridgend regatta finished in 1914, the Wembury regatta continued until 1939, well organised by Archie Nelder a farmer living at Wembury, and the river Yealm regatta. Wembury regatta had the starting and finishing line opposite the Yealm Hotel pier now demolished.

Besides the sailing and rowing races Wembury had fast outboard speed boat races up the Kitley river. These boats were 14 to 16 ft. long, mostly powered by 32 hp American Elto Quad motors and were capable of speeds close to 35 knots. Aircraftsman Shore of Mount Batten Air Station, better known as *Lawrence of Arabia*, in his white Skentelbery-built speed boat, was one of the hot competitors.

Leonard Modely, whose parents owned the beautiful schooner *Icicle*, used to show up during the regattas in his biplane diving into the valley bombing the crowds with small bags of flour with long streamer tails. Leonard survived the 1914-18 war as a fighter pilot and was later to command a Spitfire Squadron near Bolt Tail during the 1939-45 war.

The last of the sailing crabbers raced until the 1920s when cruising yachts became popular. Before 1939 there was also a mixture of sailing dinghies racing for the *Leicester Challenge Cup*. In the early 1930s the rowing races were very popular among them the almost forgotten skiff race. These skiffs were 16 ft. long, beautiful pieces of hand crafted boat building, planked in 3/16 inch thick cedar, varnished and weighing close to 50 lbs. each. The local craftsmen making these were all Noss men, Tom Algate, Elliot Hodge and Landel Leonard at the malt house.

Veterans row the first boat from the mould of the wooden *Shamrock*, a crabber.
It is in the late 1970s and Gerry Sims, cox., Joe Roach, Edgar Foster, William Hockaday and Everitt Leonard try out this new boat at the regatta but not as part of any race. It was rowed up and down the estuary seen here against a spectators' boat with people cheering their efforts.

1930s Regatta.
This scene is below the Yealm Hotel. There is a mixture of boats here from the small rowing ones in the foreground to a Plymouth steamer out for the day. No person has been recognised from this now distant decade.

Wembury Regatta.
Wembury had its own regatta which took place mainly on the Kitley river up until 1939. This is shown on the banner in this photograph dating from the 1930s. They came over to the Yealm to use the facilities and no doubt were also supported by the local folk.

In one regatta Ernest Hodge was leading in the *Nona*, built by his brother Elliot, when the support under the thwart failed. He came to a halt with his posterior breaking through the thin planking and keel which was only one inch square.

In those days competitors had to provide their own racing boats. Landel Leonard built himself a fast 14 ft. boat and Vince Hodge had Sam Mashford build him a similar one. These two were unbeatable. I must not forget Kathleen Rowe who was virtually unbeatable in the Yealm, Plymouth and Looe regattas.

In 1911 Mr. Tenney of the Yealm Hotel presented the *Greyback Cup*, the stipulation being that the race was to be rowed in crabbers and the oarsmen to be land workers. The boats and oarsmen were to represent the villagers of Noss and Newton. The stipulation was soon forgotten and the race developed into a serious contest between the two villages. Competiton was so keen that the crabbers were dried out to make them lighter. The drying made them leak and these were stopped by filling the seams with soft soap. Local youths were pressed into polishing the bottoms of the boats with black lead hoping to increase the speed of the hulls.

In the early thirties Harry Hockaday, the retired fisherman who coxed the Newton crew with moderate success, removed a strake lowering the freeboard on his boat to make her faster. The locals at the *Dolphin Inn* gave him such a ragging that he came to Noss to see Bill Leonard who sportingly loaned him the *Emma Jane*. Counting the *Thistle*, *Eagle* and *Snowdrop*, there were now only four surviving crabbers.

The racing became so competitive with fouls at the buoys that the regatta committee changed the course. The race then started at the Mouthstone Ledge passing the buoy off the baulking stores to port, rounding a buoy at Bridgend and finishing at Noss Creek.

Prior to 1939 the regattas were such big events that crews started to practice a month in advance. During the war years the 14 ft. regatta boats remained in storage and the crabbers under cliff were neglected and fell apart. There were a few mini-regattas along with garden fetes sponsored by the Yealm Hotel in the Pool to raise funds for wartime charities.

The 1946 regatta was held and as the crabbers had fallen to pieces the Navy loaned 27 ft. five-oared whalers. The sailing races gained importance with a fleet of Mayflower sailing dinghies and several 14 ft. Internationals taking part.

In 1972 the regatta committee furnished five new fibre glass rowing boats. The racing boat design by Landel Leonard some thirty-five years earlier was cleaned up and used as a plug to make the fibre glass mould. The regatta was again becoming an important event. In 1980 the 1880 built *Shamrock*, 21 ft., the last of the crabbers, was cleaned up to make the mould of a new generation of four crabbers built by Harry Hockaday at his boat yard at Membland.

The flagging Yealm regatta took on a new lease of life. Swimming races were held at the new Pope's Quay which gave a good spectator following. Popularity of the regatta has increased. Ladies are now rowing in the crabbers, swinging the 12 ft. long oars. Beside the Greyback race between the two villages there are guild and challenge races with crews from Salcombe and Dartmouth.

Due to popular demand a mini-regatta is held two weeks after the main event. This is a fun regatta held at Pope's Quay for crabbers only. A fund raiser, competitors pay £5 to enter a crew. The crews represent various trades, pubs, churches, contracting firms, football or any type of club or activity.

In 1990 there was a wager of £100 on a race. Norman Doddridge, the winner, donated the winnings to the regatta fund. Because of the popularity of the mini-regatta a competitor is only allowed to perform in one race. There are usually over 200 competitors in this regatta. The only prize offered is a half pint of bitter or shandy expertly served by John Rowsell the keeper of the keg. Following the mini-regatta there is a laying up of the crabbers in mid September.

John Hockaday, following his father's example, has been the starter for many years. Den Shepherd, Mr. and Mrs. Leonard Carter, Jack Shepherd, John Stitson, Peter and John Leonard, Harry Hockaday and Maurice Farleigh have spent most of their adult lives involved in helping to keep the regatta running.

For many years the Yealm Yacht Club at Newton Ferrers has fostered a very popular sailing regatta, the club organising distance and passage races open to all competitors. The club has dinghy parking areas and organises a series of summer races for juniors who soon become adept at sailing the tricky courses.

There are often over twenty people in their Mirrors, Toppers and Lasers racing in their life vests in all sorts of weather followed by the very efficient rescue boat. The Yealm with its steep river banks, wind shifts and fast running tides is recognised as one of the most difficult rivers to master.

Flying the Flags.
A scene from one of the regattas from the 1930s between the Yealm Hotel and Passage Woods. A motor vessel keeps a watchful eye over the rowing boats.

Internationals.
This early 1950s photograph shows four of the Internationals which raced regularly. Left to right: *San Toy II*, Bob Baker, *Tiddlywink*, Bob Andrews and Jack Shepherd, *San Toy*, Elliot Baker. The other boat is either a *Mirage* sailed by Mike Parsons or the *Avenger* sailed by John Hockaday.

Regatta Prize Giving Evening in the 1960s.
Mrs. A. L. Pallot is carefully presenting the winner's cup to Jack Tope for the Naval Whaler's race watched by Claire Gaitley, Harry Hockaday, Barbara Stevens and John Leonard. An array of cups and other prizes await winners of the other races. The presentation took place in the Womens' Institute, Newton Ferrers.

In the middle of the naval whaler's race late 1970s.
Robert Wilson, cox., is urging his crew to keep ahead in their whaler against the one behind. Crewed by Mark Wilson, Rodney Carter, Harry Hockaday, Chris Carter and Gubby Williams they strain at the oars of this heavy whaler loaned from H.M.S. Raleigh, Torpoint.

No. 3 Naval Whaler boat in the 1979 Regatta.
Close to Riverford West Road Harry Hockaday, coxswain, Martin Cawse, Michael Hockaday, Simon Cawse, John and Peter Leonard strive with spectators looking on including Mr. and Mrs. Bishop once headmaster of Newton school. Four whalers were towed from H.M.S. Raleigh each year by motor boat by John Hockaday and Everitt Leonard loaned for the two weeks of the annual regatta.

Who is in the Lead turning by the Buoy sometime in the late 1970s?
The four crews cannot be clearly identified at this point in the whaler's race; the heavy boats are turning at the buoy close to the International Paint Company's building down the estuary. The names Len Carter, Rob Wilson, Harry Hockaday and Gerry Sims have been mentioned as probably being here. The sail of a *Redwing* is in the background.

The War Years 1939-45

Before the war Noss was a quiet peaceful village. We slept the night with front doors unlocked and days and weeks slipped quietly by the church reminding us when it was Sunday and that the following day would be wash day with rows of white sheets hung on lines by noon. People daily gossiped in the small shops rarely leaving the village.

Signs of the Second World War appeared in 1938 with the R.A.F. building hangars at Collaton Cross. We expected an airfield there but a Barrage Balloon Centre was built instead. Hitler's rise to power had been front page news for years, young people jokingly greeting each other with the Hitler salute never thinking that this man would soon plunge the world into war with grievous losses and much sorrowing.

Our elders had told us about warfare in the trenches in France and we learnt about sinkings at sea from the mariners. There were many ex-servicemen living in the area who still liked to be addressed by their military title. We young people did not know what to expect if war came, we were enjoying the rural life.

Neville Chamberlain, the Prime Minister, had returned from Munich waving a piece of paper declaring "peace in our time". We showed little interest in Hitler's conquests in Europe, the places seemed so far away. Many of us at that time had never ventured more than two dozen miles from Noss. In September, 1939, soon after Germany invaded Poland and war was declared we began to realise that the enjoyable peaceable days at Noss were coming to an end. At the start the approaching turmoil was unnoticeable. Men and women were quietly drifting away to join the forces, there were no farewell parties. Their places were taken by wide-eyed evacuees most seeing Noss for the first time.

Food rationing had started. Cliff Parsons, the local warden, was enforcing the blackout, patrolling the village every evening. Bill Roach, on the ferry, was carrying many servicemen to the pubs at Noss. The early morning bus to the dockyard was running full.

The thirty-two seater Western National buses changed their seating to face each other so providing more room for standing passengers. The sixty or more passengers staggered at each gear change on the hills. The uniformed female conductresses were having to take the fares, a most unhealthy occupation.

With petrol rationing almost everyone had to use the buses. There was no bus shelter at Plymouth so long queues formed at St. Andrew's Cross in all kinds of weather dubbed "pneumonia corner". The return fare to Noss remained at 1s 6d for adults and half price for children throughout the war.

Inspection of the Local Homeguard.
This view probably records a church parade sometime in 1940 when Lady Astor, out from Plymouth, and accompanied by the Rev. Charles H. D. Grimes, inspects the turn out. It is outside of Holy Cross church and recognised are Lt. H. Kingcombe, G. Thorn and B. Baker.

Many families with their weak radios tried to receive Daventry for the latest war news. Vera Lynn was singing her sentimental songs, Tommy Handley was entertaining us with the *Itma* show and Henry Hall with the BBC orchestra. "Music while you work" was started to cheer up people on the home front doing tedious jobs in the munitions factories.

Two Newton men, Arnold Wright and Wally Austin, both in bell-bottomed rigs, were the local Navy men patrolling the Yealm in a little white motor boat, always standing, never seated. They also maintained the buoyed wire boom defence across the Bar at the harbour entrance. They were always busy often collecting their ration of "Nelson's Blood" at the bar of the *Dolphin Inn*. Victory gardens were being dug, Land Army girls were taking the places of men on the farms helping the farmers to produce more food.

We were both shocked and relieved by the miracle of Dunkirk. The L.D.V., Local Defence Volunteers, was replaced by the Homeguard as we now feared an invasion. Harry Kingcombe was the commanding officer, assisted by sergeants Joe Hisbent, Stuart Squires and Ralph Hockaday, M.M., with about fifty other ranks of all ages and professions. Dr. Bensted Smith, the medical officer lecturing on the treatment of bullet and other wounds. In the evenings we were also taught to understand and maintain our weapons.

Our armaments were two Lewis machine guns with stands, Canadian Ross 303 rifles, 1917 vintage, a short range sten gun, hand grenades and launchers and a peculiar Smith gun which looked like a drain pipe on wheels. No one was brave enough to demonstrate it.

We had drills and marches on Sunday mornings with occasional exercises against the R.A.F. at Collaton Cross. Fresh from Dunkirk we had several sergeant instructors teaching us camouflage and battle training for mobile warfare. Our defence area was from Old Cellars to Stoke where the R.A.F. regiment took over. One evening we had a call out being told that German paratroops had landed near Totnes. We were transported to our defence area but figured this to be an exercise as we were not issued with any ammunition when we assembled at headquarters at Newton.

The months of June to October, 1940, were tense. The German were massing landing barges which the R.A.F. were bombing daily. We expected to be invaded. The only action we saw was a fist fight between a Western National bus driver and an airman from Collaton Cross during an exercise. German propaganda over the radio told us that most of our navy was sunk. Lord Haw Haw even claimed that German U boats had torpedoed Drakes Island. Savage air battles raged over south-eastern England. On Sunday 15th September, 1949, the Luftwaffe lost 185 aircraft. Soon after this date the Germans started night bombing cities using a mixture of high explosives with delayed fuses and incendiary bombs. The damage was devastating. An anti-aircraft battery took over part of Worsewell farm. Nissan hits sprung up close to the gun emplacements for accommodation.

During the air raids on Plymouth decoy fires were lit on the Drive to confuse the enemy, this area being out of bounds to civilians. The first bombs at Noss landed at the top of Passage Woods and in the adjacent field. Bombs were dropped starting at the path to the rectory. Missing the village houses, a bomb exploded at the entrance to Noss Creek with several more running down the river towards Kiln Quay. Fortunately the tide was in.

Some windows were broken at Newton. Debris from the pathfield bombs broke most of the glass in Clarry Nicholson's green houses in the valley below. Jack, the son, a bomber pilot with the R.A.F., had to spend all his leave helping his parents to repair the damage. Many other bombs fell on Newton Downs. There was a large bomb crater over thirty feet across at Shallowford Creek on the Kitley river. The only casualty was a sheep. The top of the Kitley river also received many bombs, one destroying a thatched cottage in the valley at Puslinch killing a lady.

Tony Poole and his wife Winnie gave hundreds of hours of their time running a forces canteen in their home on Riverside Road. Tony had been gassed in the First World War and now breathed through a silver tube in his throat covered with gauze and he could only speak in a hoarse whisper. The canteen soon became well known to the Free French, Polish, American, Canadian, Norwegian and South African men in the area besides Australians and New Zealanders from Mount Batten Air Station who were flying their Sunderlands on submarine patrols. Tony and Win were unfortunate in the loss of their son Donald a guardsman.

For a time troops, airmen and naval personnel were everywhere. Billy Adams kept the Saturday night dances going at Newton W.I. There was a Thursday evening film show at Newton every week. We had won the Battle of Britain. The fears of an invasion had subsided. Montgomery had defeated Rommel at El Alamein and the fighting in Africa was over. The invasion of Sicily was successful but the Allied advance was halted for a time in the Anzio region of Italy. Then came D Day, 6th June, 1944. The service personnel had vanished in Noss as fast as an outgoing tide. The village seemed deserted. Men up to forty years of age were in uniform or employed in Devonport Dockyard. The women remaining at Noss had very anxious times but joyful when they received a letter or sorrowing when a telegram arrived informing them of a casualty or the loss of a loved one.

War seemed to become a way of life reading the newspapers with their small print, listening to the BBC news casts and trying to cope with the food and clothing rationing and life in general. There were set backs after the Normandy invasion at Caen, Arnhem and the battle of the bulge. Eventually the Russians entered Berlin, Hitler took his life and the war in Europe was over.

Church bells rang out most of the afternoon. My brother Alan, a bomber pilot, was on leave. When we went to the *Swan* that evening the car park was full of people wishing to celebrate but not knowing how to start. John Hockaday showed up with his accordion. Arthur Clayton, a merchant navy officer who had been torpedoed on two occasions, produced a guitar and someone arrived with a saxophone.

A welcome home card was given to all military personnel on their return at the end of hostilities in 1945.

This small orchestra headed a congo dance down through the village. Many people joined the tail end of this snake-like dance as their houses were passed. The dance ended at the last house Point side. Spirits had been in short supply for years. The *Globe* had a little beer and sherry. This was soon consumed bringing the celebrations to an early end. The tension and anxiety of the war was over. The European fighting had ended.

The next morning a few old regatta flags were hung out, the playground cleared of stones and a few races for the children were organised accompanied by a fancy dress parade and a tug-o-war. Food rationing continued, war time living was now an accepted way of life. The lifting of the blackout appeared to be the only change in the first few months of peace.

The war against the Japanese in the Pacific kept many troops and naval personnel overseas until August. The war changed village life completely. The men and women returning from the forces had to find work elsewhere. Many of the evacuee children had no homes to go to. There was a housing shortage and very little work in the Yealm area. The young demobilised had to relocate and find work elsewhere. When their parents died their low income did not allow them to maintain the family home which was eventually sold. The closeness of village life once so enjoyable was lost.

In spite of high costs the village is returning to the happy place it was over forty years ago. The only way to keep this closeness is for the local council to promote the building of reasonably priced starter homes to keep the young generation in Noss. Without them the village will die again. The young people will have to move away and Noss will become a retirement centre for wealthy people.

Victory Celebrations in 1945.
Crowds turned out for the various activities; one recorded here with Harry Warren on the penny farthing bicycle with Ron Clayton playing his guitar. Recognised in the crowd are John Wheeler, Mary Davis, Ralph Hockaday, Margaret Crocker, Esther Pearce, Cathy Reeves, Norah Neeham, John Hockaday and Cynthia Tope.

Arthur L. Clamp – the man behind the books

Arthur Leslie Clamp was a man of boundless energy with a passion for helping others, particularly through his love of history. A printer by trade, he started his career in a printing company before moving his family from Exeter to Plymouth to teach at the Plymouth College of Art and Design, where he eventually became the Head of the Printing Department.

A Devoted Family Man

Arthur with his five children.

Despite his love of teaching, Arthur prioritised his family, always making it home by 5:30pm for tea. He and his wife, Rosemary, raised five children: Susan, Angela, Elizabeth, David, and Steven. Arthur would often combine his love of family and history by taking his children on Sunday walks, encouraging them to appreciate historical monuments by taking photos or making crayon rubbings of gravestones for his books. The family home at 203 Elburton Road was a hub of activity, with a large garden, featuring a two-storey fort and a makeshift swimming pool.

A Lifelong Learner and Adventurer

Arthur's thirst for knowledge extended beyond history to a deep curiosity about the world. He was passionate about exploring different cultures, traditions, and cuisines, often taking advantage of his long summer holidays as a teacher to travel to places like India, Russia, South America, the middle east and the USA, sometimes bringing one of his children along. This adventurous spirit even influenced his home life, as seen by the short-lived family tradition of steam-cooking vegetables after a trip to Iceland.

History is a prominent feature of family days out

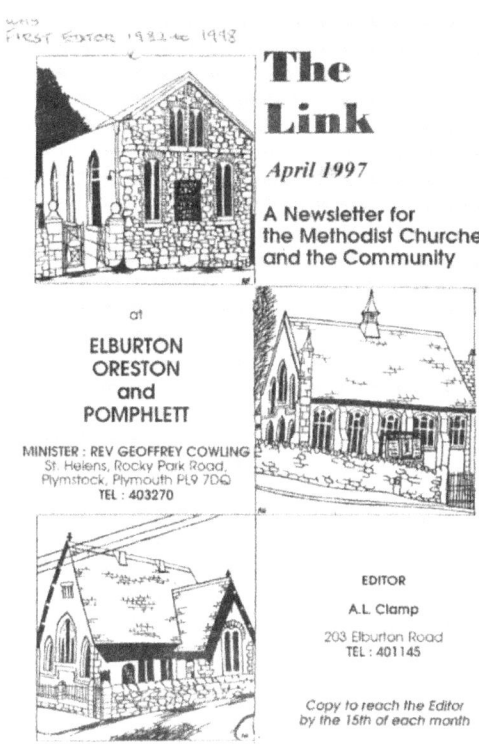

Community and Philanthropic Spirit

His commitment to serving others was evident in his long-standing involvement with the Elburton Methodist Church. He was the Sunday School Superintendent for over 15 years and served as the editor of the wider church's monthly newsletter, "The Link," for a similar duration. After Rosemary's very sad passing, Arthur later remarried and, following a chance encounter with a professor from India, established a connection with a missionary school in Chennai. Together with his new wife, Christine, he co-founded a "Sponsor a Child's Education" program that continues to this day.

*Pictured left – The cover of 'The Link' complete
with hand drawn sketches of each church by Angela
Below right – Arthur Clamp promoting his latest book
Below left – Arthur at home with his first wife, Rosemary
Below centre – Arthur on holiday with his second wife,
Christine*

A Legacy of Learning and Positivity

Arthur's greatest passion was history, which he brought to life through tireless research, documentation, and the many books he authored. He was driven by a need to "never be stuck in a rut," constantly seeking new experiences, meeting new people, and expanding his knowledge. With a positive attitude and a great sense of humour, he was always ready to help others, leaving a lasting impact on his family and community. His children, Susan, Angela, Elizabeth, David, and Steven, remember him with love and gratitude.

David Clamp, 2025

A Legacy of Local History

Below is the story of how Arthur L Clamp began writing books, in his own words, drafted shortly before he passed away in 2001. I have only made minor alterations to this text, correcting grammatical errors that he did not survive to correct himself. When I first discovered this text, I was shocked to see my name mentioned. It seems that, unbeknownst to me, I shared my first PC with him. I suspect he used it during the day when I was at school, although I do have one memory of sitting with him and showing him how it worked. It has been a pleasure to pick up where he left off and see his books republished and redistributed, and to know that I was part of the story, even back then. It was also fascinating to discover that his pricing structure matches the way I have tried to price the books, with a third going to local sellers and the rest covering printing costs with a little left over for my expenses.

I am his eldest grandson, and it is a privilege to curate his legacy, which we are calling 'The Clamp Collection'. The very last line of the text originally reads "The following pages list all the titles." Sadly, that page is missing and we have no record of all the books he published and knowing that some of those were researched by other authors makes the process of finding them even harder. I look forward to one day completing the collection and seeing them all available again. And maybe, one day, I'll even start writing my own to add to the series. For now, here is his story in his own words.

Steven Gibson, 2025

Writing and Publishing Booklets on Local Topics and Areas

I started this interest in either 1968 or 1969 when living in Woodford. I had by these dates established the Department of Printing and I think I must have been looking for something different to do. The first titles were of A5 size proofed from type set at Clarke, Doble and Brendon, Ltd., Plymouth printers, and then made up into pages and printed at Sawtell and Neilson, Ltd., Totnes.

Then began a slow process of getting them out to shops, etc. which proved to be more time consuming and difficult than actually researching, writing and getting the books into print. However, I persisted and opened a business account with Barclays Bank on the Broadway. I was advised to give it a title so I called it "Westway Publications". There came along another problem, one of storage of paper and finished books which was solved when the family moved to Elburton in 1970.

I changed the printer to Penwell, Ltd., Callington, Cornwall, as he was then just setting up himself and his prices seemed very reasonable. I did not get any of the printers to make up the complete books. I hand folded the flat printed sheets, stitched the books on a small manual table stitcher and trimmed them in a small hand turned guillotine which I bought from someone in Penzance for £40. It was brought up in a van.

The trouble and time going to and fro to Callington was too much so I transferred the printing to PDS Printers, Prince Rock, Plymouth, and I have been with them ever since. Now they are at Plympton which is easy to reach and they fold the flat sheets which was turning out to be a long chore which only saved a small part of the printing costs.

All my first titles were written by myself. I took the photographs and developed them in the loft of the house, the type was set by now on a computer situated in the house at Elburton from which I had collected photographic lengths of text to cut up and law down as pages.

At some point I decided that I would do my own film processing of lith film so I bought a large second hand process camera from Kingsbridge and learnt through trial and error to make line negatives of the text and halftone negatives of the illustrations which proved more difficult than I anticipated. The main problem was trying to keep the developer in the large dish at the correct temperature as any change would affect the developing time. I replaced this old camera with a brand new one bought from Croydon, Surrey, costing £900. This has turned out to be a great asset cutting out an expensive part of the printer's costs and one crucial aspect of the work which I could control.

By the middle 1970s there were many outlets I had contacted in Plymouth, up to Dartmoor, Exeter, around to Torbay, Totnes, Dartmouth and the South Hams. The market for local books was much greater than I had first thought and through getting to know many local people undertaking research themselves had the chance to help and make up books for other people who had in most instances, got together a collection of photographs with some text in a rather muddled way. Through my experience in print I was able to shape up their work and get it into print and in every case I had to pay the printer and let the person have the royalties. In the majority of titles produced in this manner this was another way of producing titles and it did give some profit to my work. However, I must say that in a few cases I lost out by either the other person getting the numbers wrong, not returning any monies from stock I delivered or they thought that more of their books should have been sold.

The print run was usually 1,000 copies and from time to time I have had reprints of 250 copies. It took about ten years to clear the first print run so I always had large stocks in the garage, workshop, etc. The numbers sold during the early years was about 7,000 copies a year increasing to around 9,000 copies and for the whole of the enterprise about 500,000 have been sold. The booklets have become part of the local scene and many people collect them, shops regularly order copies and I go around certain areas month by month restocking or replacing titles as necessary.

During the past year or so I have started setting the text on a Packard Bell PC, something which I should have done some years back. I share it with Steven Gibson, my grandson. There appears to be no end to the market for local books, but I could not earn a regular income because of the long time it takes to sell stock.

However, now exceeding 100 titles made up mainly of A4 twenty-four page booklets, some folded guides, with selling prices set with a third going to the shop which is the trade custom, the original idea has been quite successful and could go on for ever.

Apart from monetary benefits, however spasmodically these might be, I have learnt a lot myself, met many interesting people and have become part of the local scene with requests to give talks and to advise people about getting into print.

Arthur L Clamp, 2001

Death of local historical author

'He was an incredible character who was just loved by everybody who knew him'

A WELL-loved Elburton author has died at the age of 68.

Arthur Clamp (pictured right), who was one of the West Country's most successful writers, died at St Luke's Hospice, Turnchapel, after losing his battle against cancer.

Tributes have been flooding in for a man who was known in the community as a prominent writer and outgoing person.

He produced more than 140 titles during his life, dealing with both fiction, fact and history, often discussing West Country topics that were close to his heart.

One of his most acclaimed books was *The Plymouth Blitz*, and he also won credit for *The Rise and Fall of the Bearings of Membland Hall*, set in Noss Mayo.

He achieved sales of between 7,000 and 9,000 books every year and it is estimated that he has sold over half a million books, covering the areas of Plymouth, Dartmoor, Exeter, Torbay and the South Hams.

Mr Clamp was born in Mitcham, Surrey, in 1932, and was the eldest of four children.

He moved to Devon in 1941 to avoid the London air-raids.

Mr Clamp trained as a printer in Exeter and also gained a teachers' certificate in 1959 from Garnet College in London.

Plymouth College of Art, however, was to prove to be Mr Clamp's working home for the following 32 years until 1991, when he retired as head of the printing department.

He had a great interest in travel and had visited the USA, Tanzania, China, Russia, Peru, as well as travelling across Europe, where he presented talks and slide shows on his experiences as a writer.

Mr Clamp was a member of Elburton Methodist Church for many years, superintendent of the Sunday school and editor of the church newsletter, as well as being involved in much charity work.

He was president of the Plymouth and District Field Club and an active member of the Elburton Residents' Association.

He enjoyed leading walks on Dartmoor and historical tours throughout the West Country.

Mr Clamp married his first wife, Rosemary, in 1956 and they had five children – Susan, Angela, Elizabeth, David and Steven – and she died in 1987. He also had 11 grandchildren.

He leaves a wife Christine, after remarrying in 1991, and her two children and three grandchildren.

'He was an incredible character who was just loved by everybody who knew him,' said his wife.

'He will be missed by his family, his friends, the people he worked with and just everybody who knew him through his books.'

More than 300 mourners attended his funeral at Elburton Methodist Church on Monday.

The attendance was a celebration of his life – he would have found that really special. It shows his vibrancy and love of people,' said Mrs Clamp.

Steven Clamp added that his father was 'a well respected and loved man, missed by a great many people throughout the South West and far beyond'.

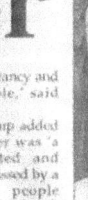

This newspaper article, published by the Evening Herald on 17th August 2001, forms a good record of his life. Just as he encourages us to learn more about local history, we encourage you to learn a little about him. For that reason, we have included these pages at the back of all the most recently republished books, in honour of his memory and recognition of his contribution to the community.